# Cockatoos

A Complete Cockatoo Pet Guide

Cockatoo Facts & Information, where to buy, health, diet, lifespan, types, breeding, fun facts and more!

By Lolly Brown

D1198352

# Foreword

Cockatoos have been around since the 17th century! These birds are native in Indonesia and had been kept as pets since the 1850's!

Cockatoo parrots were admired by bird enthusiasts because of their intelligence and affectionate qualities. Many pet owners believe that with Cockatoos there's a lot more than meets the eye! These birds are full of surprises and they love to show off!

Although Cockatoos are truly a great choice as pets, these birds doesn't come with a thin instruction manual. But fear not! In this book you'll be easily guided on understanding your Cockatoos, their nature, their behavior and characteristics, how you should feed and care for them and a whole lot more.

Embark on a wonderful journey of sharing your life with a Cockatoo Parrot. Learn to maximize the great privilege of living with one and be able to share this unique and unforgettable experience just like the many pet owners that came before you!

# Table of Contents

Chapter One: Introduction...................................................1

Chapter Two: Meet Cockatoos ...........................................11

Facts about Cockatoos .........................................................12

Quick Facts .........................................................................14

Cockatoos in History............................................................15

Popular Types of Cockatoos ................................................17

Chapter Three: Cockatoo's Requirements ............................21

Pros and Cons of Cockatoos ................................................22

Cockatoos Behavior with Other Pets...................................23

Ease and Cost of Care ..........................................................24

**Initial Costs**........................................................................24

**Monthly Costs** ...................................................................27

Chapter Four: Tips in Buying Cockatoos.............................31

Restrictions and Regulations in United States ...................32

Permits in Great Britain and Australia................................34

Practical Tips in Buying Cockatoos ....................................34

How to Find a Cockatoo Breeder .......................................35

Local Cockatoos Breeders in the United States.............36

**Local Cockatoos Breeders in Great Britain**.....................45

Selecting a Healthy Cockatoo .............................................45

Chapter Five: Maintenance for Cockatoos............................47

Habitat and Environment ........................................48

   a.) Ideal Cage Size for Cockatoos ...................48

   b.) Cage Maintenance...................................49

Diet and Feeding ..................................................56

   a.) Nutritional Needs of Cockatoos ...............57

   b.) Types of Food .......................................57

   c.) Toxic Foods to Avoid..............................65

Handling and Training Cockatoos........................66

   a.) Trimming Your Cockatoo's Nails.............69

Basic Cockatoos Breeding Info ...........................74

The Cockatoo Breeding Process .........................75

Hybridization of Cockatoos................................78

Chapter Seven: Keeping Cockatoos Healthy.......89

Common Health Problems..................................90

Recommended Tests ..........................................105

Signs of Possible Illnesses.................................106

Chapter Eight: Cockatoo Checklist .....................109

Basic Information...............................................110

Cage Set-up Guide ............................................111

Nutritional Information.....................................112

Breeding Information.........................................112

Do's and Dont's ................................................113

Index..................................................................................125

Photo Credits.....................................................................131

References...........................................................................124

# Chapter One: Introduction

The name, "Cockatoo" is derived from an Indonesian word called *"kakak tua"* which means "older sibling." The Indonesian root name was also used as terms for the family and generic names – *Cacatuidae* and *Cacatua* respectively Cockatoos have a reputation for being very inquisitive and affectionate! Its vibrant appearance goes along with its enthusiastic attitude, and that's what kept these birds unique throughout the ages!

Aside from its attractive and beautiful array of colors and mutations, just like other birds, Cockatoos also have an outgoing personality and they are very intelligent in nature. They are very fond of playing and hanging around people and they love to cuddle – be warned because you might find yourself hugging them all the time, it's quite addictive.

They are parrots that are classified under the family of *Cacatuidae*; these birds are scientifically known as *Cacatua Vieillot*. Later on in this book, you will learn more about the different types and species of Cockatoo parrots so that you can choose what is best for you!

Cockatoos are great as pets, though sometimes some people may find them quite naughty and aggressive because these birds are very active by nature and could be way talkative at times, but that's of course, part of who they are. They are clever and can be easily trained and they can do various tricks as well! Although, Cockatoos are generally easy to care for, you will still need some useful tips, so that you can maximize its true potential.

Compare to other bird species, Cockatoo parrots live for a long time; the oldest cockatoo recorded reached 100 years old! These birds have an average lifespan of 30 - 60 years! But, if you take good care of them, they will certainly live longer than you might expect. They're friendly and charming companions, and because of that you need some guidance on how to take care of them, raise them and possibly learn how to be like them as well as teach them to be like you!!

Fortunately, this ultimate guide will teach you on how to be the best Cockatoo owner you can be! Inside this book, you will find tons of helpful information about Cockatoo Parrots: how they live, how to deal with them and realize the great benefits of owning one!

*Glossary of Important Terms*

**Abdomen -** bottom part of the bird

**Alula -** three feathers springing from the base of the primaries

**Axillary** - ventral area between the body and the wing

**Birdhouse** - another name for a nest box, or a home for a bird

**Blood Feather** - any feather which still has a blood supply to it

**Breast -** front part of the chest

**Breast band -** stripe across the breast

**Breast spot -** small, differently colored area on the breast

**Breeding Cycle** - time period beginning at nest building through egg laying and raising young to the point of independence

**Breeding Plumage** - referring to the colorful plumage which the males of many species acquire for the breeding season

**Brood** - young of a bird that are hatched or cared for at one time

**Carnivorous** - flesh-eating birds

**Cap -** top of the crown

**Cere -** fleshy area between the beak and face

**Cheek -** area of head below eye and above the neck

**Chest -** front part of the body

**Chick** - a young or new born bird

**Chin -** part of the face below the bill

**Closed Band** - a completely closed ring of metal that can only be put on a bird within a certain time, usually from 8-10 days in a small bird and up to four weeks in the larger species of birds. The bands are usually imprinted with hatch date and place of origin

**Clutch** - total number of eggs laid by a female bird in one nest

**Collar** - rear portion of crown

**Colony** - group of birds nesting together in close association

**Comb -** colored area over eye found in males

**Crest -** tuft on the head

**Crop** - a sac inside a bird where its neck meets the body. It holds food before digestion

**Crown -** top of the head

**Dimorphic** - a species is dimorphic when there are distinct visual characteristics between the genders

**Dispersal** - movement of a young bird from the site where it hatches to the site where it breeds

**Diurnal** - occurring or active in the day

**Domestic Bird** - a bird that has been bred within the country

**Downy Plumage** - refers to the plumage of a chick upon hatching

**Dihedral** - wings of a flying bird held at an angle appearing to form a "V"

**Ear patch** - area around ear opening

**Eye line** - line of feathers in front of and behind the eye

**Eye ring** - pale-colored feathers encircling the eye

**Eyebrow** - line of feathers above the eye

**Facial discs** - rounded, earlike areas on the face

**Field Mark** - a characteristic or combination of characteristics such as color, shape, or specific marking (eye rings, wing bars, breast stripes), by which a species of bird can be distinguished from other species

**Flank** - area between the belly and the wings, more posterior

**Flank stripe** - band on the flanks

**Flight feathers** - primaries and secondary's on the wings

**Forehead** - part of the face above the eyes

**Frugivorous** - birds that feed primarily on fruit

**Gorget** - iridescent throat feathers on a hummingbird

**Granivorous** - birds that eat grains or seeds

**Greater secondary coverts** - feathers overlying bases of secondary

**Grit** - small pieces of rock, shell, or other hard substances that birds eat to help them digest other foods. Grit helps grind up coarse vegetable matter

**Hand Fed Bird** - The babies are taken from parents at about two weeks, and then fed by people

**Head stripes** - bold lines on the head

**Hindhead** - rear portion of crown

**Horns -** paired contour feathers arising from head

**Inner primaries -** group of primaries closest to the body

**Inner secondary -** group of secondary closest to the body

**Inner wing -** shoulder, secondary and secondary coverts

**Jizz -** the abstract combination of a bird's posture, plumage, pattern, shape, size and behavior

**Karyotyping -** a method of telling the gender which is non-invasive. A drop of blood is taken from the bird, usually by pulling out a blood feather

**Lore -** area between the eye and the bill

**Lower mandible –** lower part of the bill

**Malar stripe -** area at the sides of the chin

**Mantle -** upper surface of the wings and the back

**Migration -** an extended journey a bird makes from one place to another

**Molting -** the process by which a bird renews part or all of its plumage by shedding old, worn feathers and growing new ones

**Monomorphic -** both genders of the bird appear identical.

**Mustache -** area at the sides of the chin

**Nape -** back of the neck

**Neck patch -** inflatable sac on neck used by males in courtship display

**Nestling -** young bird that has not left, or abandoned, the nest.

**Niche -** the role a bird plays in the ecosystem, including what it eats and where it lives

**Occiput -** rear portion of crown

**Open Band -** this type of band, which is squeezed shut around the bird's leg is indicative of an imported bird.

**Order -** taxonomic group above the level of family but below that of class. Orders are composed of one or more families.

**Ornithology -** science of birds

**Outer primaries -** group of primaries farthest from the body

**Outer secondary -** group of secondary farthest from the body

**Outer tail feathers -** part of the tail farthest from the center

**Outer wing -** alula and primaries

**Pinnae -** projecting feathers

**Plumes -** large, conspicuous, showy, feathers

**Preening -** the process by which a bird cleans, arranges, and cares for its feathers, usually by using its bill to adjust and smooth feathers

**Primaries -** flight feathers attached to the "hand"

**Primary coverts -** feathers protecting and covering the primaries

**Quarantine -** a period of isolation required for new or imported birds

**Rictal bristles -** stiffened feathers near bill

**Roost -** a place where a bird sleeps, sometimes in groups

**Ruffs -** fringe of feathers growing on the neck

**Rump -** area between the upper tail coverts and the back

**Scapulars** - area of feathers between the back and the wings

**Secondaries** - flight feathers attached to the "elbow"

**Secondary coverts** - feathers protecting and covering the secondaries

**Shoulder** - feathers overlying bases of median secondary coverts

**Side** - area between the belly and the wing

**Spectacle** - eye ring and supraloral line together.

**Speculum** - highly colored area on secondaries of several ducks.

**Subterminal band** - stripe before tip of tail.

**Tail** - feathers extending from the rear of the bird.

**Tail coverts** - under and upper tail coverts.

**Tarsus** - part of the leg between the knee and the foot.

**Taxonomy** - the way bird scientists classify bird species based on their similarities to or difference s from one another

**Terminal band** - stripe at tip of tail

**Tertiaries** - feathers adjoining the secondaries

**Throat** - front part of the neck

**Throat patch** - front part of the neck

**Tibia** - part of the leg above the knee

**Underparts** - belly, undertail coverts, chest, flanks, and fore neck

**Undertail coverts** - feathers covering underside of base of tail

**Underwing** - underside of wing

**Upper mandible** - upper part of the bill

**Upperparts** - back, rump, hindneck, wings, and crown

**Uppertail coverts** - feathers covering upperside of base of tail

**Upperwing** - upperside of wing

**Weaned Bird** - a bird that is out of the nest, and eating on its own

**Whisker** - area at the sides of the chin

**Wing bars** - pale tips of secondary coverts creating a stripe on wings

**Wing coverlets** - primary and secondary coverts, or feathers overlaying others

**Wing lining** - median, lesser and marginal coverts on underwing

**Wingspread** - distance from tip to tip of the longest primary feathers of the outstretched wings

**Wing stripe** - paler area at base of flight feathers

**Wing pit** - between the body and the wing

**Wrist** - area at base of the primaries

**Zoonosis** - a zoonosis is any disease of animals that can be contracted by a human being

# Chapter Two: Meet Cockatoos

Cockatoos often referred as "cacato," "crockadore," "cokato," "cocatore," and "cocatoo" especially during the 18th century, are very enchanting birds to care for that comes in various sizes and colors. These birds are also considered as one of the most famous parrots. Cockatoos are very ideal pets especially for first time bird owners. But before getting a fascinating parrot as your pet, it's very important that you know what it is inside out! Like many other things, you need to have proper knowledge and invest a significant amount of time to truly study and understand where these birds are coming from.

That is how you will determine if this kind of pet is the right choice, so that you know what you are dealing with.

On the next sections, you'll be introduced to the smartest and one of the most popular parrots in the world. Prepare to meet Cockatoos!

### Facts about Cockatoos

Cockatoos, which are scientifically under the Subfamily of *Cacatuinae,* are birds that are native to shrublands, woodlands, rainforests and alpine forests in Australia, Indonesia, Papua New Guinea and Philippines. These birds life expectancy is about 30 – 60 years or more!

These birds have an enthusiastic and sociable attitude towards people, which makes them an interesting choice as pets.

These parrots had been popular since the 17th century especially when scientists brought it to Europe.

In the wild, Cockatoos are relatively medium to large birds with variety of colorful feathers such as white, pink, grey, yellow, black, and because of color mutations they are now available in cinnamon, silver, and grey and white with flashes of other colors.

Aside from talking, they are also fond of chewing, napping and playing interesting games to keep them from being bored and also to satisfy their curious minds. They are totally cool and have a knack for a fun time!

Most Cockatoos are generally easy to train and can be well-behaved as long as you provide them with adequate attention, interaction, and love. They can easily become part of the family and a loving companion if you are willing to put in the time and effort to take care of them.

Cockatoos have relatively the same features with other parrot species. These birds have short legs, strong claws and a waddling gait including a curved beak shape and a zygodactyl foot. The Cockatoos species have different erectile crest and they have strong large bills with a less brightly colored plumage.

Their average size including tails is about 12 – 24 inches, and weighs 300 grams – 1,200 grams. It has an average lifespan of 30 – 60 years. The maximum recorded lifespan of a Cockatoo is 100 years.

In terms of their behavior and personality, they are quite notorious for screaming out loud and they are very noisy. They will destroy and chew on any objects available, requires lots of interaction and can be quite aggressive to unfamiliar faces. But they are primarily easy to tame and train and they are very friendly once they get to know you.

These parrots are omnivorous and usually feed on seeds, insects, fruit and nuts. Cockatoos are not sexually dimorphic; they need to undergo through DNA sexing to determine their gender, although some bird enthusiasts claims that they can determine a female cockatoo through their eye iris.

In terms of reproduction, Cockatoos reach their sexual maturity around 3 to 5 years old and breeding period usually occurs between August and January; females' clutch size ranges from an average of 2 – 3 eggs and incubation lasts for about 25 – 30 days.

Just like any parrots, Cockatoos can be trained to mimic human speech and imitate other sounds by using their bifurcated trachea, which are equivalent to vocal cords in humans.

**Quick Facts**

- Taxonomy: phylum *Chordata,* class *Aves,* order *Psittaciformes,* family *Cacatuidae,* subfamily *Cacatuinae,* Genera *Prosciger, Callocephalon, Nymphicus, Calyptorhynchus, Eolophus, Lophochroa, Cacatua*
- **Distribution**: Australia, Indonesia, Papua New Guinea, Philippines, and the Solomon Islands
- **Habitat**: Shrublands, woodlands, rainforests, alpine forests

- **Lifestyle**: Flock Oriented
- **Anatomical Adaptations**:
- **Breeding Season**: between August to January
- **Eggs**: 2 – 3 eggs
- **Incubation Period**:  – 25 - 30 days
- **Sexual Maturity** : 3 – 5  years old
- **Average Size**: 30 cm – 60 cm (12in – 24 in)
- **Average Weight**: 300 g – 1,200 g (0.66 lb – 2.65 lb)
- **Coloration**: white, pink, grey, yellow, black; different color mutations
- **Sexual Dimorphism**: not sexually dimorphic
- **Diet**: Seeds, Insects, Fruit, Nuts (Omnivore)
- **Sounds:** Vocal Communicator, Screamer
- **Interaction:** Highly Social
- **Lifespan**: 30 –  60 years

## Cockatoos in History

Cockatoos was discovered and acquired by European sailors around 1850 from Indonesia and other eastern countries that they had explored like Philippines, Papua New Guinea, and the Solomon Islands. Cockatoos had been kept as pets by natives of these regions as well.

Also during the 1800's, sailors or explorers not just brought alive cockatoos back in Europe but also dead specimens of other parrots for scientists and collectors to examine.

In 1900 birds became very popular and a common pet by Europeans particularly the aristocrats at the time. All of these pets were imported from the wild. Scientists and bird enthusiasts were fascinated by these colorful creatures and some Europeans also started learning how to breed parrots like Cockatoos, later on they also learned how to create different color mutations that are now almost applicable in every parrot species.

In 1985 the first Cockatoos were captive bred in the Netherlands. During that time, significant milestones in terms of breeding Cockatoos were achieved especially in the United States and United Kingdom.

Around 1995, Cockatoos became popular as ever; almost all cockatoos are now captive bred. Several wildlife organizations and group efforts aimed in protecting the cockatoo populations in the wild have been established and government laws also protect the birds from importing diseases. As of now, it is illegal to import certain cockatoo species according to CITES appendix.

Today, the bird continues to be a very popular pet, people actually prefer buying baby cockatoos now than adult ones, and because of that, the amount of unwanted adult cockatoos is growing. Cockatoos are perfect for families with children and a very gorgeous cuddly companion that you can count on.

## Popular Types of Cockatoos

In this section, you will be provided with a list of the most popular Cockatoos that are readily available in pet stores and ideal as pets. There are lots to choose from and it'll be a just a quick and easy read of these marvelous species. You will learn all of the ideal Cockatoo pets, their major characteristics, and their colors. Read on!

**Palm Cockatoo**

Also known as the Goliath Cockatoo, these birds have red facial marks and they appear as big black birds. It is not known to be among the most affectionate Cockatoo species but it is the most well-known species of all the black cockatoos.

Black Palm Cockatoos requires solid training which is why it is recommended for very experienced bird owners because they need plenty of interaction. They love to scream out loud and are not a good choice for those who can't tolerate loud noises and therefore not suited for people who live in apartments or condominiums.

**Citron-crested Cockatoo**

They have a reputation for being more quite than most Cockatoos, and they are classified as a subspecies of the Lesser Sulphur-Crested Cockatoo. The only difference between the two is that the crest of the citron-crested cockatoo is orange instead of yellow and it also has a yellowish cheek mark. These birds are highly recommended for pet owners who have plenty of free time to spend with their pets because they are highly sociable type of birds.

**Goffins Cockatoo**

These birds have big personalities wrapped up in a small package. They are small white birds with flashes of pink-orange and yellow feathers. They are known for being sweet and interactive on top of it, they are very low maintenance.

**Moluccan Cockatoo**

Also known as the Salmon-Crested Cockatoo, these birds are one of the most famous cockatoo species. They are very cuddly birds that form strong bonds with their owners. They are quite clingy because in the wild, Moluccan Cockatoos live in large flocks, which may explain their inherently social nature. Their crest when erected is bright orange in color; these birds also have an impressive yet intimidating look and they are quite huge when it reaches its maturity.

## Sulphur-Crested Cockatoo

They are one of the bigger species of Cockatoos. In terms of appearance, they are quite colorful because it has white feathers with a yellow crest and flashes of yellow feathers under its wings not to mention its black beak and feet. The feathers of its crest are pointy and loose-fitting, and even if it's down, it is still quite visible.

Sulphur Crested Cockatoos have a reputation for being loud and noisy birds, yet very sweet and affectionate like other Cockatoo species. It is also an exceptional pet because it can be taught to learn new tricks, can mimic human speeches and have a variety of great behaviors. Like any other birds, they're also very active, so if you're looking to acquire this bird, get ready for one incredible loud but awesome pet!

## Umbrella Cockatoo

They are known as the gentle giants in the cockatoo species; they are huge in size but are gentle, sweet and docile in their attitude which makes them great companions. In terms of appearance, they have a white crest with patches of bright yellow on the inner side of its wings. They are not aggressive, unless of course it's threatened, despite of its intimidating appearance and size. They are also highly sociable and forms strong bonds with their owners.

## Rose-Breasted Cockatoo

Also known as the Galah Cockatoo is one of the smaller species of Cockatoos that has a very distince appearance; these birds' chest is bright pink, the wings are light grey and the crest is whitish pink. They are native in Australia and are usually found in the wild forests.

These birds have are very friendly and sweet in nature but also quite sensitive. They need plenty of love and lots of human interaction, otherwise they might get depressed. They are getting very popular as pets but it is advisable that as a potential owner you make sure that these birds do require lots of attention and therefore not suited for everyone.

# Chapter Three: Cockatoo's Requirements

Are you now thinking of getting a Cockatoos? No problem! After learning what Cockatoos are, where they come from, how they live and its different types, it's time to give you practical tips on what you need to know before buying one.

In this chapter, you will get a whole lot of information on its pros and cons, its average monthly costs as well as the things you need so that you will be well on your way to becoming a legitimate Cockatoos pet owner -should you decide to be one! It's up to you! Read on!

## Pros and Cons of Cockatoos

The information listed below is the advantages and disadvantages of owning Cockatoos:

**Pros**

- **Personality:** They are intelligent, humorous, active and affectionate
- **Appearance:** Vibrant and vividly colorful
- **Abilities:** Very easily trained, can mimic human sounds and perform tricks
- **Impact on Humans:** They are very intelligent, down-to-earth and loves to interact with people; great long-time companions

**Cons**

- **Cost:** They are quite expensive depending on how large the parrot specie is
- **Noise:** They are sometimes too talkative and loves to scream out loud
- **Damage to Your Home:** They love to chew up and destroy your wooden furniture if left out of the cage
- **Behavior:** They can be nippy or aggressive at times especially towards strangers.

## Cockatoos Behavior with Other Pets

There is actually no general rule when introducing your pet parrot with other types or species of birds, sometimes they'll get along, sometimes they won't.

Fortunately, Cockatoos in general are very welcoming to other species regardless of its kind! They are very friendly parrots, and you as the owner don't have to worry if ever you would introduce them to other birds or pets, they love to hang out with everyone including people!

There is however a flipside, Cockatoos tend to be harmful companions for smaller birds or pets such as guinea pigs or rodents because these small animals can fall as prey with their strong beaks, which could be fatal. Even if your Cockatoo gets along with a larger or smaller bird, accidental injuries can occur during play or when they are just simply spending time inside the cage. So keep a tight watch over them especially if you just introduced them or if they interact with other species.

It is also best to socialize your Cockatoo while they are still young, because they are still vulnerable and can be very accepting of other members once they get used to it.

As a general rule, you can introduce other types of birds but do so with caution so that they could easily warm up with their new feathered friends.

Unlike other birds that are highly individual,

Cockatoos love to be in flocks when they're in the wild or even in captivity. It'll be easy to train them to like other parrots, though sometimes they can be a bit witty.

Experts also suggest that the best behaved Cockatoos are those who were exposed to lots of change in the environment and the ones who were trained to socialize with people, because they become more adjusted.

## Ease and Cost of Care

Owning a Cockatoo parrot is quite expensive because it's very popular and it also depends on the size of the bird and keeping one may give you a tight budget. The supplies needed in keeping one will definitely add up to your daily life expenses, if you want to keep Cockatoos as a pet you should be able to cover the necessary costs it entails.

In this section you will receive an overview of the expenses associated with purchasing and keeping a Cockatoo as a pet.

## Initial Costs

The initial expenses associated with keeping Cockatoo as pets include the cost of the bird itself as well as the cage, cage accessories, toys, and grooming supplies.

You will find an overview of these costs below as well as the estimated total expense for keeping a Cockatoo:

**Purchase Price: starts at $800 - $4,000**

As established earlier Cockatoos come in all sizes, from small to medium to large size birds, they are one of the most popular breed of parrots that's why it can be quite expensive! The purchase price also depends on the color of the bird; some Cockatoos with rare color mutations or is a show quality of breed could be more expensive than others.

The general rules in these birds are, the more colorful, rarer and clever it is, the more expensive it can be. So better check your budget to see which Cockatoo is best for you.

**Cage: starts at $249 - $2,499**

The bigger, the better! Even if you own a small size Cockatoo, it's a general rule for birds that they live in cages where they could have the luxury of space, after all that is where they're going to spend most of their time right? So pick the right cage for your Cockatoos, so that they'll enjoy life like you!

**Accessories: estimated $100 in total**

If you bought a cage, you'll definitely need cage accessories like perches, lights, feeding dishes, stands, cage covers and harnesses for your Cockatoos. Accessories can be quite expensive depending on the brand as well as the quality and size of your purchase. Cockatoos are like other

birds have a naughty side too, they'll chew everything!
Watch out!

**Toys: more or less $50 in total**

Cockatoos love to play and chew lots of toys! They
will easily destroy any toy that came there way, which
usually means that you may need to keep buying more
often. Like other parrots, they need plenty of stimulation to
keep their intelligent and curious minds entertained. The
price of the toys depends on the brand you choose to buy.
Keep birdie boredom at bay with chewable toys for your
Cockatoo.

**Grooming Supplies: more or less $50 in total**

As part of pet hygiene, your feathered friend needs to
be cleaned and properly groomed. There are lots of
grooming supplies that you can buy online or in your local
pet store. Again, the brand and quality of the product affect
the price range to keep your Cockatoos clean and healthy.

| Initial Cost for Cockatoos | |
|---|---|
| **Cost Type** | **Approximate Cost** |
| Purchase Price | $800 - $4,000 (£653.97 - |

| | |
|---|---|
| | £3269.84) |
| Cage | $249 - $2,499 (£203.55 - £2042.84) |
| Accessories | $100 (£81.75) |
| Toys | $50 (£40.87) |
| Grooming Supplies | $50 (£40.87) |
| **Total** | $1,249 - $6,699 (£1021.01 - £5476.17) |

*Please note that these amounts are computed at the starting price and converted at the current exchange rate, which is $1 = £0.82. Costs may vary.

## Monthly Costs

The monthly costs associated with keeping a Cockatoo can be quite expensive even if they are generally low maintenance. Some of the things that needs to be bought on a monthly basis like food supplements, cleaning materials and even veterinary care every now and then will definitely add up to your expenses. Below are the estimate monthly costs it entails.

**Bird Food (seeds, pellets, treats, fruits, vegetables, etc.): approximately $50 - 60 per month**

Your Cockatoos needs a varied and healthy diet. There's a massive selection of high quality seed diets, complete food and pelleted foods to choose from both online and in your local pet stores, not to mention some treats you might want to buy especially when they're doing tricks! The cost will depend on the brand as well as the nutritional value of the food.

Feeding a variety of these foods, alongside fruits and vegetables is the key to a healthy parrot.

## Cleaning Supplies: at least $10 per month

You don't need brand new cleaning supplies every month, but of course, you will run out of bird shampoo and soap eventually. Just include it in your budget.

## Veterinary Care: starts at $150 - $1,000 or more

Cockatoos rarely get sick compared to other types of parrots, but it's important to keep them healthy by taking them to an avian vet for medical check-up every now and then. Avian vets are trained specifically to work with exotic birds whereas a general practicing vet may not be familiar with their needs and treatments especially if they are sick, not to mention the medicines needed.

If in case, this happens it's better and wiser to set aside a portion of your budget for any medical needs that will come up.

**Additional Costs: at least $10 per month**

In addition to all of these monthly costs you should plan for occasional extra costs like repairs to your Cockatoos cage, replacement toys, food supplements, medicines etc. You won't have to cover these costs every month but you should include it in your budget to be safe.

Here is the overview of your total monthly expenses for the needs of your pet Cockatoos.

| Monthly Costs for Cockatoos | |
|---|---|
| **Cost Type** | **Approximate Cost** |
| Bird Food | $50 - $60 (£40.87 - £49.05) |
| Cleaning Supplies | $10 (£8.17) |
| Veterinary Care (optional) | $150 - $ 1,000 (£122.62 - £817.46) |
| Additional Costs | $10 (£8.17) |
| **Total** | $220 – 1,080 (£179.84 - £882.86) |

*Please note that these amounts are computed at the starting price and converted at the current exchange rate which is $1 = £0.82. Costs may vary.

# Chapter Four: Tips in Buying Cockatoos

If you are still interested in reading this chapter, that only means one thing: you have already decided to buy a Cockatoo. Good choice, they are really down-to-earth, friendly and awesome birds, you'll surely enjoy being with them!

Here you will learn tips and tricks on how to select healthy Cockatoos, where to find the right breeder as well as the laws and permit you need to be aware of before buying.

## Restrictions and Regulations in United States

If you are planning to acquire a Cockatoo as your pet, then you have to think beyond the cage. There are certain restrictions and regulations that you need to be aware of, because it will not only serve as protection for your bird but also for you. Here are some things you need to know regarding the acquirement of Cockatoos both in United States and in Great Britain.

### a.) What is CITES?

CITES stands for Convention on International Trade in Endangered Species of Wild Fauna and Flora. It protects Cockatoos by regulating its import, export, and re-export through an international convention authorized through a licensing system.

It is also an international agreement, drafted by the International Union for Conservation of Nature (IUCN), which aims to ensure that the trade in specimens of wild animals and plants does not threaten their survival.

Different species are assigned in different appendix statuses such as Appendix I, II or III etc. These appendices indicate the level of threat to the current population of the bird with consideration to their likely ability to rebound in the wild with legal trade.

## b.) Appendix I and II of CITES

Some birds are considered potentially endangered or highly threatened as indicated in CITES' Appendix I while some are not (Appendix II). In this section, you'll learn the differences between the two appendices and how to get the permits necessary.

Appendix I simply means that the birds included on this list are most likely endangered species and may require import or export permit to prevent illegal trading.

Most species of Cockatoos are listed on Appendix II, which means that they are not necessarily threatened with extinction but are still vulnerable in becoming endangered. International trade may be granted an export permit or certificate and no import permit is required for the species listed in Appendix II, although some countries make require such permits for safety purposes.

The Division of Management Authority processes applications for CITES permits for the United States. You should allow at least 60 days for the review of your permit applications.

For more information on how to apply for a CITES permit please visit their website at: <http://www.fws.gov/international/cites/>

## *Permits in Great Britain and Australia*

In Great Britain and Australia you may need a permit for you to be able to import, export, or travel with your Cockatoos. This permit is called an **Animal Movement License**.

Aside from the CITES permit, sometimes a Pet Bird Import License and a veterinary health certificate are required before bringing your bird in Great Britain, the purpose of this is to prevent the spread of diseases if the bird is a carrier.

You can apply for a Pet Bird Import License through this link: <http://AHITchelmsford@animalhealth.gsi.gov.uk.>

Like in the United States being aware of the regulations and getting a license is an important thing you need to consider before you acquire, import or export a bird. This does not only protect the animals but it can also avoid confiscation of your pet.

## *Practical Tips in Buying Cockatoos*

Now that you are already aware and have prior knowledge about the legal aspects of owning a Cockatoo, the next step is purchasing one through a local pet store or a legitimate breeder.

Here are some recommendations for finding a reputable Cockatoo parrot breeders in United States and in Great Britain.

### How to Find a Cockatoo Breeder

The first thing you need to do is to look for a legit avian breeder or pet store in your area that specializes in Cockatoos.

You can also find great avian breeders online but you have to take into consideration the validity of the breeder. It is highly recommended that you see your new bird in person before buying anything on the internet. You can find several recommended list of Cockatoo local breeder websites later in this book.

If possible, spend as much time as you can with your prospective new Cockatoos before buying it. Interact with the bird and see how it is with you.

Continue the diet of the bird as advised by the store owner or breeder to maintain its eating habits. Look for any health problems or issues as well.

Finally, only purchase a Cockatoo that is banded. Banding means the bird have a small metal band on one of its legs placed at birth by the breeder which is inscribed with the bird's clutch number, date of birth and the breeder number.

Leg bands are indicators that the purchaser and the bird itself are in the country legally and have not been smuggled.

## Local Cockatoos Breeders in the United States

Here are the lists of available Cockatoo breeders in the United States. Availability and costs of these Cockatoos may vary over time, please check the links provided for any updates.

### Birdman's Baby Parrots

5668 N Lincoln Ave Chicago, Illinois

Website: www.birdmansparrots.com

Tel. No.: 773-317-3785

### AJ'S Feathered Friends

804 N. La Fox Street. South Elgin, IL 60177

Website: www.ajspetshop.com

Tel. No.: 847-695-5624

### Something Cheeky

Clayton, North Carolina 27520

Website: www.somethingcheeky.com

Tel. No.: 1-919-585-2241

### In A Pickle Parrots

7924 Broadview Road, Broadview Heights, Ohio 44147

Website: www.inapickleparrots.com

Tel. No.:  440-627-6477

Email:  Inapickleaviary@aol.com

## World of Birds

15 Perry Street, Chester, New Jersey 07930

Website: www.worldofbirds.com

Tel. No.: 908-879-2291

Email: worldofbirds@optonline.net

## Morning Glory Birds

West Hempstead, New York 11552

Website: www.facebook.com/glory.birds.7

Tel. No.: 516-972-3860

## Featherheads

Port charlotte, Florida 33948

Website:http://www.birdbreeders.com/breeder/13627/feathe rheads-florida-port-charlotte-FL

Tel. No.: 813-679-4961

## Ginos Exiotic Birds

Blue Jay, CA 92317

Website: http://www.birdbreeders.com/bird

Tel. No.: 176-095-604-66

Email: Gmorrialle@gmail.com

## Fancy Feathers

31 Roseland Avenue, Caldwell, New Jersey

Website: www.fancyfeathersaviary.com

Tel. No.: 973-403-2900

E-mail: ddargenio@gmail.com

## The Bird Lady

17044 I-20, Lindale, Texas 75771

Website: http://www.birdbreeders.com/breeder/7816/the-bird-lady-east-of-dallas-off-of-i-20-TX/reviews

Tel. No.: 956-309-0750

E-mail: debinmcallen@att.net

## SpringOak

Dripping Springs, Texas 78620

Website:http://www.birdbreeders.com/breeder/5561/springoak-dripping-springs-TX

Tel. No.: 512-630-1626

Email: sherylcoffman1@gmail.com

## The Parrots Nest Of Maryland

4508 G Lower Beckleysville Road, Hampstead, Mary Land

Website: http://www.birdbreeders.com/bird/

Tel. No.: 410-374-1636

Email: livesaybrian@aol.com

## Linville's Aviary

Miami, Florida 33174

Website:http://www.birdbreeders.com/breeder/2920/linvilles
-aviary-miami-FL

Tel. No.: 305-968-1536

E-mail: cerbyu@aol.com

## Avian Events, LLC

Conyers, GA 30094

Website: www. avianevents.com

Tel. No.:  770-500-2882

Email: tom@avianevents.com

## The Parrots Nest Of Maryland

4508 G Lower Beckleysville Road, Hampstead, Mary Land

Website: http://www.birdbreeders.com/bird/

Tel. No.: 410-374-1636

Email: livesaybrian@aol.com

## Green Parrot Superstore

8165 S. State Rd, Goodrich, Michigan

Website: www.greenparrotsuperstore.com

Tel. No.:  810-636-9120

Email: greenparrotsuperstore@gmail.com

## Thea's Parrot Place

Fallbrook, California 92028

Website: www.theasparrotplace.com

Tel. No.: 760-842-3436

Email: theasparrotplace@att.net

## Tail Feathers

Durand, Illinois 61024

Website: http://www.birdbreeders.com/breeder/38015/tail-feathers-durand-IL

Tel. No.:  815-248-4035

Email: tgsmall49@live.com

## Birds By Joe LLC

1309 Bound Brook Road, Middlesex, NJ 08846

Website: www.birdsbyjoe.com

Tel. No.: 732-764-2473

Email: service@birdsbyjoe.com

## Above the Rainbow Aviary

Gallipolis Ferry, West Virginia 25515

Website:http://www.birdbreeders.com/breeder/10444/above-the-rainbow-aviary-gallipolis-ferry-WV

Tel. No.: 304-812-4340

Email: abovetherainbowaviary@comcast.net

## Tweety Bird Aviary

263 Hobbs Island Road, Huntsville, AL 35803

Website: www.tweetybirdaviary.com

Tel. No.: 256-656-2019

E-mail: LBroach487@Gmail.com

## Whidbey Birds

P.O. Box 1682 Coupeville, Washington 98239

Website: www.whidbeybirds.com

Tel. No.: 360-929-2869

E-mail: whidbeybirds@msn.com

## Birds Exotic

1060 S. Chester Ave. Delran, NJ 08075

Website: www.thebirdstore.com

Tel. No.:  856-764-2473

E-mail: thebirdstore@yahoo.com

## Lone Palm Aviary

Loxahatchee, Florida 33470

Website: www.lpbirds.com

Tel. No.: 570-730-1366

Email: jessica@lpbirds.com

## The Finch Farm Co.

Miami, Florida 33101

Website: www.thefinchfarm.com

Tel. No.: 877-527-5656

E-mail: jenna.thefinchfarm@gmail.com

## Ara Aviaries California

Agoura Hills Los Angeles, California

Website: www.aracaris.com

Tel. No.: 805-338-3549

Email: billysaylors6@gmail.com

## Ana's Parrots

East Stroudsburg, PA 18301

Website: https://www.facebook.com/PoconoAna

Tel. No.: 646-496-5005

E-mail: poconoana@yahoo.com

## Parrotsrok

Skiatook, Oklahoma 74070

Website: http://parrotsrok.com/Home%20Page.html

Tel. No.: 918-289-8787

E-mail: mandmok@sbcglobal.net

## The Parrot's Cove

New Iberia, Los Angeles 70560

Website: theparrotcove.com

Tel. No.: 337-519-3943

E-mail: theparrotscove@theparrotcove.com

## 5 Oaks Aviary
Oklahoma City, Oklahoma 73150

Website: www.fiveoaksaviary.com

Tel. No.: 405-209-4312

E-mail: fiveoaksaviary@msn.com

## Debbie's Birdhouse
32 East Harrison Street Tunkhannock, Pennsylvania 18657

Website: www.debbiesbirdhouse.com

Tel. No.: 570-240-7268

E-mail: Debbie57@ptd.net

## Pet Paradise
35535 Euclid Avenue, Willoughby, Ohio

Website: www.petparadiseohio.com

Tel. No.:  440-942-9016

E-mail:info@petparadiseohio.com

## The Bird Hut
Nashville, Tennessee 37221

Website: www.the-bird-hut.com

Tel. No.: 615-739-0631

E-mail: midtnecho@yahoo.com

## Delorce's Bird Barn
Charleston, South Carolina 29429

Website: www.delorcesbirdbarn.com

Tel. No.: 8432161553 or 8438198618

Email: brendabrinson1234@gmail.com

## Toucan Jungle

Vista, CA 92084

Website: www.ToucanJungle.com

Tel. No.: 760-672-0127

Email: Chris@Toucanjungle.com

## Bill and Kennys family birds

135 Terry Road Hartford, Connecticut 06105

Website: http://www.birdbreeders.com/breeder/26465/bill-and-kennys-family-birds-hartford-CT

Tel. No.: 203 441-0366

Email:billsbirdsnbeaks@gmail.com

## Kedzie Parrot Place

East Lansing, Michigan 48823

Website: www.kedzieparrotplace.com

Tel. No.: 517-204-3878

Email: kedzieparrotplace@hotmail.com

## Cindy's Parrot Place

Chesapeake, Virginia 23321

Website: http://www.cindysparrotplace.com

Tel. No.: 1-844-572-7768

Email: info@cindysparrotplace.com

## Local Cockatoos Breeders in Great Britain

Here are the website links and contact details of local Cockatoos breeders in Great Britain:

### UK Breeder Websites

### Hand Reared Parrots
<http://www.handrearedparrots.co.uk/>

### Bird Trader
<http://www.birdtrader.co.uk/>

### PreLoved
<http://www.preloved.co.uk/>

*Selecting a Healthy Cockatoo*

Cockatoos on average can live for up to 30 - 60 years and more! These birds are long time companions, and its longevity highly depends on how your chosen breeders took care of them especially when they were young.

This section will give you simple tips on how you can spot a healthy Cockatoo that you can keep for life!

**a.) Signs of a Healthy Cockatoo**

Look out for these signs so that you know if your prospect bird is healthy:

- The bird should be active, alert, and sociable
- It should eat and drink throughout the day
- It should have dry nostrils and bright, dry eyes
- The beak, legs, and feet should have normal appearance
- It should have a dry and clean vent
- Its feathers should be smooth and well-groomed

# Chapter Five: Maintenance for Cockatoos

Assuming that you have already bought a Cockatoo as your pet, the responsibility that comes with it is the most crucial part of the process. You as the owner, have to provide for its basic needs so that it will be healthy and happy. In this chapter you will learn the different requirements needed for your bird such as its cage, accessories and food necessary for the maintenance of your Cockatoos.

## *Habitat and Environment*

Cockatoos have adapted well to human-modified habitats, such as parks and gardens in villages and towns. Like other kinds of birds, Cockatoos should be kept in a bird-safe environment. As the owner you need to have knowledge of its habitat requirements and environmental conditions to ensure that your bird is healthy. You will find tons of information in this section regarding the maintenance your pet needs in order to keep them happy.

**a.) Ideal Cage Size for Cockatoos**

Cockatoos, like other birds, love lots of space when it is inside its cage. A general guideline that you can follow when it comes to bird cages is that, the parrot should not have restricted movements and should be able to flap its wings without touching the sides of the cage.

It is also advisable to buy a durable cage preferably with locks to prevent them from escaping because they are naturally curious and quite naughty at times.

The cage should ideally provide room for both horizontal exercise and vertical climbing. A minimum of 27"x 27"x39" (70x70x100cm) with 1 inch (4 - 5 mm) bar spacing is the recommended cage size for Cockatoos.

It is also advisable that the cage material uses non-toxic paint or else it can cause your pet to be poisoned by metal.

It shouldn't also be made out of brass either because it contains zinc which could kill your parrot as well.

Ideally the cage should also have at least three doors. One as the main entrance and the other two should be used for food and water.

Your bird will be spending most of their lives inside the cage that's why it needs to be large so that it can also accommodate lots of toys and perches.

## b.) Cage Maintenance

Your parrot's cage could affect the health of your pet so it's very important that you check it daily for any dirt, like its feces and spoiled food left in perches and cups to prevent health problems.

You should also change the cage paper every other day as well as check the metal parts & bars of your bird's cage periodically for chipped paint and rust, because your bird will most likely chew or swallow the flaked pieces.

You should be able to clean the cage thoroughly at least once every month. You could use a mild dishwashing liquid or bleach with warm water for about a minute. Then rinse all soap and bleach thoroughly with water before letting your bird inside the cage.

## c.) Location of the Cage

Finding the perfect cage is just as important as knowing where to place it. As established earlier, Cockatoos are not just fond of screaming, they love to scream out loud! So keep that in mind and take that into consideration when finding a good location for your bird.

Put them in a place where they'll get to interact with people, and won't be too much of a disturbance at the same time – if in case they scream non-stop, and they will!

Put the cage at an eye level to create a sense of confidence in your bird and place the cage in a higher location so that they would feel secure just like in the wild.

Avoid placing the cage near dangerous fumes or drafts, this might kill them. Do not also place it directly in a window because the sun can cause your parrot to become ill due to too much heat. If it helps you can at least find a shade or cover for the cage, so that your bird may get just the right amount of heat during the day and feel comfortable during night time.

Finding the right location of the cage could lessen stressful situations for your bird so that they can enjoy their life with their new owner.

## d.) Recommended Supplies

Now that your cage is all set and you already have an idea on where to properly place it, you need to provide supplies to meet its needs. Here are the recommended supplies that your Cockatoos needs:

## Perches

The main purpose of perches is to exercise your bird's feet; it could also prevent sores and foot related health issues in the future. In the wild, birds like Cockatoos, are used to transferring from one tree to another but in captivity of course they can't do that, so a great alternative is to buy them perches, preferably made out of fresh fruit tree branches. The minimum area for the perch is about ¾" - 1" (2 - 2.5 cm) in diameter.

You can buy different types of perches such as wood dowel, natural branch type, a therapeutic perch or a cement perch as well as Eucalyptus branches; just make sure that it is not poisonous.

Cockatoos also love to gnaw perches, and because of that you may have to replace it regularly. There are lots of perches you could choose from especially from online stores. These perches could also be used as ropes and swings for your pet. Do not put the perch above the bird's bowl or dishes otherwise the food and water will be contaminated.

## Toys

Cockatoos are very playful and active and like any other birds, they will chew anything, you may find yourself regularly buying and replacing new toys to keep them happy. It is recommended that you purchase toys that are easy to be destroyed, it'll be very interactive for your Cockatoos to prevent boredom. However, if you're in a tight budget, you can also buy toys that are durable so that it could last longer. There are a lot of toys online and in pet stores that you can buy for your Cockatoo.

It is not advisable to put all of the toys inside your bird's cage because it will become dirty and overcrowded. Rotate the toys at least once a week.

## Dishes

Buy at least 3 sturdy dishes; one for fresh water, one for pellet or seed mix and one for fresh foods. Avoid buying plastic dishes because your Cockatoos will most likely break it and it could also be harmful to its health. Place it away from the perches so that it would not be contaminated with bird droppings.

## Formulated Diet

Some Cockatoos owners feed their birds only with seeds, while some only provides a pellet diet; this however could limit the nutrients your pet is receiving.

Experts suggest that parrots should be given a variety of food for a balanced nutrition or what they call a formulated diet.

Cockatoos are a very energetic and lively parrot that's why a good combination of formulated diet (seeds, fruits and vegetables) as well as a good amount of protein and other nutrients plus clean water is essential to keep their bodies healthy and active.

You will need a good supply of packaged pellet diet, to be mixed with seed. Then you can slowly add fresh foods and protein. Formulated bird food may already contain vitamins so it's not recommended that you give another one separately unless prescribed by your vet. Conversion takes about a week or so depending on your bird and how well you feed them.

## Treats

Cockatoos can also be taught to perform different kinds of tricks and should undergo "bird training," but of course, it always comes with a price! You can give your pet different types of treats such as fruits, seed and spray as well as Do-It-Yourself (DIY) treats like pretzels, popcorn or something healthy that your bird can munch on. Later in this book, you will be provided with a list of recommended treats as well as treats you should avoid.

## e.) Bird Bath for Cockatoos

Cockatoos unlike other birds don't need a regular bath, they are clean by nature and they preen themselves regularly, ideally you can bathed them on a weekly basis in the morning, to maintain a good skin condition. Here are some things you need to know on how to maintain your bird's hygiene and keep a healthy life.

Provide a misting bottle or a birdbath. All birds should be gently misted with a water bottle at room temperature. The spray should be sprayed up over the bird much like a shower rain, never spray the bird directly in its face.

It's important that you keep an eye in your bird while it is bathing. Bathe your Cockatoo with clean water. Distilled water is sometimes required. Speak to your veterinarian on the best choice of water for your bird. During its misting and bathing procedures, make sure there are no drafts because it can cause respiratory issues. It may chill your bird when he is wet. Use towels and blankets, but be careful because it can catch the bird's nails and beaks in their threads.

To ensure that the oils from their skin glands, disease organisms or items such as lotions and hand creams do not transfer to your bird's feathers, wash your hands with soap and water thoroughly before handling your Cockatoo.

Your bird may be ill if it seems to stop grooming and becomes dirty. Once you see this signs, contact your avian veterinarian immediately.

**f.) Lighting and Environmental Temperature**

The average room temperature for your Cockatoos should be anywhere between 65-75°F (18 - 24°C). Also avoid drafty areas that will get direct heat from sun for any portion of the day.

Parrots also have tetra-chromic vision (4 color light vision including ultraviolet), that's why a full color light bulb must be present in the cage area. The incandescent or monochromatic light bulbs usually found in households are not a good choice for your Cockatoos.

Cover the cage during nighttime or at least provide a shade to block out any excess light and also creates a more secure sleeping place. Be careful when using fabrics as cover because your bird might rip it with its claws or beak and could likely eat it.

Never ever place the cage in the kitchen or somewhere near cooking fumes because bird's can be very sensitive, that even a small amount of smoke can be fatal.

## Diet and Feeding

In the wild, Cockatoos primarily eat palm nuts, seeds and fruits. Since these birds are very active, they will need nutrients that are rich in calories, protein and fats among others.

Fortunately, today's supplements have opened new and healthy options for pet owners. In this section you will be guided on how to properly feed your parrot and learn the feeding amount and nutritional requirements they need.

## a.) Nutritional Needs of Cockatoos

Feeding your Cockatoos is not that complicated. However, its level of activity should be taken into consideration to meet its nutritional diet. They're not choosy eaters but like what was mentioned earlier, it is highly recommended that parrots should be given a variety of food for a balanced nutrition.

As much as possible avoid only giving the same type of food such as a pellet diet or seed diet only; it can result in nutrient deficiency and may lead to diseases due to its limited nutrients, which could also shorten the life expectancy of your parrot.

This section outlines the foods your pet will appreciate in order to meet the majority of its dietary needs.

## b.) Types of Food

### Seeds and Pellet

Seeds are a big part of any bird's diet; they eat seeds naturally in the wild and it is also a good source of Carbohydrates. However, seeds alone can cause complications because it is naturally fatty. Although some Cockatoos need fatty acids for their skin development, it still should be moderated. It is not advisable that you mixed seeds with pellets and feed it off right away, although a lot of people do recommend that; for best results offer seeds first for a few days, then slowly incorporate pellets into the diet until your Cockatoo gets well adjusted.

The key is to give it in moderation. Feed them at least 1/8 - 1/4 cup of fortified parrot mix or diet, the amount may vary depending on how much your Cockatoo can consume.

## Fresh Vegetables

Vegetables contain phytonutrients that enhance the body's immune system which prevents illnesses. Veggies are also a rich source of natural fiber for the body. However, keep in mind that you should feed them with vegetables in moderation to prevent diarrhea and make sure they are properly washed before feeding it to your bird.

Below is the list of highly recommended vegetables for Cockatoos:

- Artichoke
- Asparagus
- Beets and greens
- Broccoli and greens
- Cabbage
- Carrots
- Cauliflower and greens
- Celery
- Chard
- Chickweed

- Chicory
- Chinese Cabbage
- Cucumber
- Dandelion Greens
- Edamame
- Eggplant
- Fennel and leaves, stems, seeds
- Kale
- Leeks
- Lettuce ( darker is better)
- Mustard Greens
- Okra
- Peas/Snap Peas/String Beans/Snow Peas
- Peppers (all types)
- Radicchio
- Radish and greens
- Spinach
- Sweet Potato/Yam (cooked/parboiled)
- Squash (all types)
- Tomatoes (offer in moderation)
- Turnips and turnip greens
- Watercress
- Wheat Grass
- Yams

## Fruits

Fruits are healthy and sweet; they also provide natural sources of sugars for the parrots. It is recommended that you only offer bite-sized fruits and do remove the pits or seeds of the fruits to prevent your Cockatoos from choking.

Below are list of fruits that are highly recommended by veterinarians for your Cockatoos:

- Apples (no seed)
- Apricots (no seed)
- Banana
- Blackberries
- Blueberries
- Cherries (no seed)
- Coconut (feed sparingly due to fat content)
- Cranberries
- Custard Apple
- Dragon Fruit
- Figs
- Guava
- Grapefruit
- Grapes
- Kiwi Fruit
- Lemon
- Lime
- Longan
- Lychee

- Mango (no seed)
- Melon (cantaloupe, watermelon, honeydew)
- Nectarine (no seed)
- Olive (fresh)
- Oranges
- Papaya
- Passion Fruit
- Peach (no seed)
- Pear (no seed)
- Pineapple
- Plum (no seed)
- Pomegranate
- Pomelo
- Quince
- Raspberries
- Rose Hips
- Rowan Berries
- Schizandra Berries
- Starfruit
- Strawberries
- Tamarillo
- Tangerine

**Important Reminder:**

Offer fruits and vegetables daily or every 2-3 days. As a caution, if your Cockatoo didn't consume all the fruits you gave, remove all of its traces from the cage to avoid the risk of eating a spoiled fruit.

## Vitamins

As mentioned earlier, some fortified parrot diet or parrot mix already contains essential vitamins. Before buying a good pellet mix or picking vegetables for your Cockatoos, you should keep in mind that Vitamin A is one of the most essential vitamin birds need.

Vitamin A improves vision and can also boost immunity. Eggs and meat are good sources of Vitamin A as well as different types of vegetables like carrots, kale broccoli, sweet potatoes, cantaloupe and squash. Too much or not enough of Vitamin A can potentially leave your Cockatoos vulnerable to diseases. Since Cockatoos aren't all the same, it is best to consult with your avian veterinarian first to know the right amount of Vitamin A your pet needs.

## Amino Acids

Cockatoos need high levels of protein or amino acids to build their tissues, feathers, muscles and skin. Birds in general can produce their own amino acids.

However, there are some amino acids such as threonine, tryptophan, leucine, lysine, methionine, phenylalanine and valine that some Cockatoos are not able to produce or sustain in its body. Fortunately, the sources of these essential amino acids are available in today's bird diet products.

Here is the list of recommended protein for your pet Cockatoos to feed on:

- Beans (cook small amounts as needed)
- Chicken (cooked, preferably shredded not fried)
- Eggs (cooked/hard boiled)
- Nuts (all types)
- Peanuts
- Seeds (birdseeds provide protein)
- Sprouts
- Turkey (cooked, preferably shredded)
- Meal Worms (feed it occasionally)

## Calcium

Calcium's primary role is to make bones grow stronger and it also allows calcification of eggshells in birds. In captivity, you can provide calcium in the form of a cuttlebone or calcium treat that is attached inside your bird cage. You can also offer a powdered supplement such as packaged oyster shell which can be added directly to your pet's food. Follow the instructions on the supplement package. Calcium is also vital for muscle contraction, blood clotting and heart functions.

It is optional that your Cockatoos be exposed to UVB light for at least 3-4 hours a day; this may help for its optimal physiologic use of the calcium you are giving to your bird.

## Water

Hydration is just as important for birds as it is for human beings especially during hot weather conditions to avoid dehydration; Cockatoos may drink 10 times its normal water intake during summer. They should be given access to clean, fresh and cool water. Do not use tap water because can cause the bird to be ill, as well as distilled water, instead use unflavored bottled drinking water or bottled natural spring water. If in case, tap water is used, treat it with a de-chlorinating treatment. Inability to provide fresh water to pet birds can cause upset stomach with unbearable stomachache.

Water is vital to maintain cells, digestion, feathers, and metabolism.

All water given to birds for drinking, as well as water used for misting, soaking or bathing must be 100% free of chlorine and heavy metals.

## Treats

As mentioned earlier, you could give your parrots a reward every time they do something right like performing tricks or simply learning how to speak. You can feed them with different types of nuts such as almonds, macadamias, and walnuts. You can also give easy to digest and bite-sized fruits or Do-It-Yourself treats every now and then.

Some examples of DIY treats are carrot muffins (minus the sugar), popcorn, corn, unsalted pretzel sticks with fruits and brown rice with berries. They will surely love something appetizing to eat and this is also a positive reinforcement for the bird especially during training them.

### c.) Toxic Foods to Avoid

Some foods are specifically toxic for your Cockatoos or any type of birds in general. Make sure that your bird never gets to eat one of the toxic items below and ensure that an avian veterinary checks your bird every now and then. These harmful foods is as important as selecting the right supplements and food items for your bird.

The following list of foods is highly toxic for your Cockatoos:

- Onions
- Alcohol
- Mushrooms
- Tomato Leaves

- Caffeine
- Dried Beans
- Parsley
- Chocolate (highly allergic)
- Avocados
- Junk Food
- Apple and Cherry Seeds
- Lettuce
- Milk and Dairy Products
- French fries,
- Marbled meat
- Peanut Butter
- Butter

## Handling and Training Cockatoos

There would be instances that your pet will be out of its cage, especially for Cockatoos. These birds are very active and naturally playful and outgoing. However, it's also important to keep in mind on how to properly handle and train your Cockatoos so that it will not cause harm to itself and to people as well.

In this section, you'll learn some guidelines on how to confidently handle your parrot as well as some tips on trimming its nails, wings and beaks to maximize its balance, abilities and flying potential.

## a.) Tips for Taming Your Cockatoos

Taming your Cockatoo is the first thing to do before teaching them some cool tricks.

The flipside of owning a Cockatoo is that they have quite a reputation for being a bit mischievous, in some cases they even tend to bite when feel threatened. The key is to figure out the level of your bird's comfort zone and remove it so that you could have a great bonding experience together. Here are some tips on how to do tame your Cockatoo:

- Start by slowly touching your parrot in its beak. Carefully move your hand closer and closer towards its beak. If the parrot reacts or moves away, stop for a while.
- Wait for it to calm down, then take your hand away and give a treat.
- Practices repeating this procedure until you are able to fully touch its beak. Your Cockatoos will eventually tolerate you in touching its beak and once you do, you can also scratch their beak. Just be extra careful when doing it, their beaks are sharp and really strong, but you have to conquer your fear if you want to get along with them!

**b.) Tips for Training Your Cockatoos**

Now that you and your Cockatoo quite get along already, strengthen your relationship by training them some basic lessons.

Training a Cockatoo is not that hard to do, in fact it can be a fun and rewarding bonding experience for you and your feathered friend! There are lots of pet owners out there who have properly trained and raised a well-behaved Cockatoo. They are clever creatures by nature, that is why they can absorb information very quickly and easily as long as you do it right.

Trust is the most important key in training your parrot. The first thing you need to do is to be able to establish a solid connection and rapport between you and your pet.

This section will provide some guidelines you can follow in getting your bird well behaved and disciplined. Are you ready? Read on!

Stepping Up is a basic skill your parrot should learn, to find out how to do this follow the tips below:

- A good way to pacify your bird into your hands without being forceful is to try and make your parakeet step up onto a handheld perch.

- Slowly and progressively begin training it to step up on your hand. If you are afraid of being bitten then wear gloves, but you may want to get rid of it eventually because it might still encourage them to bite you because they can chew the leather.
- Hold your hand in a short distance away from your parrot so that when it tries to step into the target stick, it will have no choice but to step into your hand.
- Keep practicing until your parrot won't need your stick anymore. It will get accustomed and comfortable whenever you command it to step up in your finger

## Grooming Your Cockatoos

### a.) Trimming Your Cockatoo's Nails

Like many parrots, Cockatoo have a sharp, needle-like nails because they do a lot of climbing in the wild, and they also use these nails to dig into wood to keep them secure.

Unclipped nails can dig into the skin, leaving scratches or painful wounds to a person, only clipped to a point that the bird can perch securely and does not bother you when the bird is perched on your hand. Many people have their Cockatoo's nails clipped to the point that it becomes dull and the bird can no longer grip a perch firmly.

This can result to becoming more clumsy and nervous because it cannot move without slipping. This nervousness can develop into fear biting and panic attacks.

Another tip is only use a styptic powder on your bird's nails, not the skin!

**b.) Trimming Your Cockatoo's Beaks**

Although, Cockatoos can pretty much maintain its beak's from deformity on its own, it's still important that you keep them in good condition. They are very fond of chewing and pecking everything they can get into. That's why it may eventually become dull which could also lead to deformation if not properly cared for.

Consult a qualified veterinarian to show you the proper way in trimming your pet's beaks. You can also check out several grooming items such as lava and mineral blocks that are available in your local pet store, to keep their beaks in great shape.

**c.) Clipping a Cockatoo's Wings**

Birds are design to fly, young Cockatoos can be fairly clumsy and flying gives them confidence as well as agility, stamina, and muscle tone.

Before clipping their wings, make sure that your Cockatoos are flying, maneuvering and landing well already. If they do not learn how to properly land by lifting their wings and flaring their tail, then when they are clipped, they could injure themselves and could also break their beak or keel bone.

Consult a qualified veterinarian to show you the proper way in clipping a bird's wings. A certain amount of flight feathers will be removed while leaving the smaller balancing feathers inside the wing closer to the body uncut.

# Chapter Six: Breeding Cockatoos

If you decided to buy two Cockatoos, for instance a male and female and keep them together, you should definitely prepare for the possibility of breeding, unless it's the same gender, otherwise you're going to be caught off guard! If you are interested in breeding your Cockatoos, this chapter will give you a wealth of information about the processes and phases of its breeding and you will also learn how to properly breed them on your own. This is not for everyone but if you want to have better understanding about how these birds procreate, then you should definitely not miss this part! On the contrary if you are interested in becoming a reputable breeder, then this is a must read chapter for you.

## Basic Cockatoos Breeding Info

Before deciding if you truly want to become a breeder, you should at least have prior knowledge on their basic reproduction process and breeding. This section will inform you on how these creatures procreate.

**a.) Sexual Dimorphism**

Cockatoos are not sexually dimorphic; some bird enthusiasts can determine the gender of the cockatoo through the eye coloration.

Female birds have a red colour eye iris that turns into red-brown after two years, which helps to somehow determine the sex of the bird.

However, for the purpose of being accurate, it is best that your bird go through DNA analysis, which uses sample blood or feathers. Although, some breeders claim that they can distinguish if the bird is male or female because of its features, it is still indefinite unless it's DNA is tested.

DNA Sexing or Surgical Sexing can also provide additional information on its sexual maturity and capability to reproduce. It is inexpensive and convenient so if you like to know more about your bird's sexuality you should definitely give it a try. Some veterinarians might also try chromosomal analysis on your macaw to determine its gender.

## b.) Mating and Reproduction

Cockatoos are typically monogamous when it comes to finding its mate. The breeding period for these birds usually occurs from August to January and once they start breeding, they'll continuously breed every year.

In terms of reproduction, Cockatoos reach their sexual maturity as early as 6 months old; females' clutch size ranges from 2 – 3 eggs with a maximum 4 - 5 eggs and incubation lasts for about 25 - 30 days.

The chicks become independent and leave the nest in when they reach approximately 60 - 100 days.

It is highly recommended that you provide an additional 20% increase on fatty seeds as well as their intake of vitamin supplements and proteins such as hard-boiled egg and shredded chicken during the breeding process.

It's also important to note that the incubation temperature should be kept between 37.2° - 37.3 °C (99.1°- 99.2°F) and humidity level should be at about 50 – 55% before the eggs are hatched.

### The Cockatoo Breeding Process

In order to have a clear sketch of how Cockatoos reproduce, this section will show you the breeding process and the information you need to know, so that your pets can successfully procreate.

## a.) Selecting Cockatoos for Breeding

For you to select a healthy, fertile and active parrot it is recommended that your parrot undergoes clinical examination by a veterinarian. This is essential to determine if your parrot is capable of reproduction or not and at the same time it can prevent diseases that could be transmitted to the coming flock.

## b.) Setting up a Good Nesting Environment

Cockatoos in the wild usually nest in tree hollows or cliff openings; in captivity, you need to set up a nice environment to replicate that natural breeding and dwelling place so that they can successfully mate and create healthy clutches. The nest box size for a small-size cockatoo should ideally measure 12" wide x 31" high or
(30 cm x 80 cm); for a medium-sized cockatoo should ideally measure 14" wide x 39" high (35 cm x 100 cm); while large-sized cockatoos 18" wide x 59" high (45 cm x 150 cm)

Keep in mind that the box should be three times the size of your Cockatoos. It is highly recommended that the nest box is wide so that your Cockatoos can have lots of space to move around and that it should ideally be made out of oak wood or metal.

The nest box should have a circular or round entrance hole that has an opening of about 4 inches (10 – 12 cm) for small birds; 4 inches to 5 inches (10 – 12 cm) for medium-sized birds; and 5 inches to 6 inches (12 – 15 cm) for large Cockatoos.

Make sure that a strong wire is attached to the outside walls of the nest to prevent from escaping. To be able to help stabilize the eggs you can add about 2 inches of suitable nest box litter at the bottom of the box. Providing this may also be beneficial in absorbing the droppings from the chicks

## c.) Nesting Materials

If you prefer to build your own nest box instead of buying one, you have to make sure that the materials you use are strong so that it will have a good foundation otherwise, your Cockatoos could easily destroy it.

You should also put short pieces of wood or wood chips inside the box for your birds to chew; you can also give them bite-sized timber. Just make sure that it is large enough to not let the small chicks accidentally ingest it. This may help the breeders increase the percentage of fertile eggs and synchronize their breeding cycle as well.

## d.) Brooding and Incubation

Cockatoos breed all year round but breeding season usually happens around August to January. Smaller species of Cockatoos reach their sexual maturity around 3 to 5 years old; females' clutch size ranges from 2 – 3 eggs with a maximum 4 - 5 eggs and incubation lasts for about 25 - 30 days.

Generally, there is a 1 – 2 days interval for female Cockatoos after the first egg is laid. The chicks become independent and leave the nest in usually in 2 – 3 months or approximately 60 – 100 days.

### e.) Hatching

On average, the eggs hatch in about 24 – 48 hours after the incubation period for Cockatoos and it takes about 2– 3 months before the young Cockatoos leave the nest. Consult your vet on the suitable type of diet and vitamins or supplements needed for your baby Cockatoos.

## Hybridization of Cockatoos

Hybrids are the offspring of parents of different species, subspecies or races. Cross-breeding is quite common especially within genera. Hybrids are a wonderful mixture of colors and they have interracial qualities, which makes it way more expensive than regular Cockatoos, so it's favorable for pet traders.

Generally, there are three generations of hybrid in parrots; the first-generation hybrid is a crossing of two natural occurring species. The second-generation hybrid is a natural Cockatoos specie combined with a first-generation hybrid, while the third-generation hybrid is the product of crossing hybrid Cockatoos (either first or second generation).

Some bird enthusiasts and experts are against the practice of hybridization because it affects the naturally occurring bird population. If you would like to breed a hybrid Cockatoos, it is best to consult with your avian veterinarian first to check if your parrot has the capability to reproduce and to also avoid diseases.

### a.) List of Hybrid Cockatoo Breeders in United States

Below are the lists of hybrid Cockatoos breeders in United States, please be reminded that these Cockatoos may be more expensive than their usual price. The rarer the species, the more expensive it could be. The availability and prices of these birds may also vary.

### Green Parrot Superstore
8165 S. State Rd, Goodrich, Michigan

Website: www.greenparrotsuperstore.com

Tel. No.:  810-636-9120

Email: greenparrotsuperstore@gmail.com

### Thea's Parrot Place
Fallbrook, California 92028

Website: www.theasparrotplace.com

Tel. No.: 760-842-3436

Email: theasparrotplace@att.net

## Tail Feathers

Durand, Illinois 61024

Website: http://www.birdbreeders.com/breeder/38015/tail-feathers-durand-IL

Tel. No.: 815-248-4035

Email: tgsmall49@live.com

## Birds By Joe LLC

1309 Bound Brook Road, Middlesex, NJ 08846

Website: www.birdsbyjoe.com

Tel. No.: 732-764-2473

Email: service@birdsbyjoe.com

## Above the Rainbow Aviary

Gallipolis Ferry, West Virginia 25515

Website:http://www.birdbreeders.com/breeder/10444/above-the-rainbow-aviary-gallipolis-ferry-WV

Tel. No.: 304-812-4340

Email: abovetherainbowaviary@comcast.net

## Tweety Bird Aviary

263 Hobbs Island Road, Huntsville, AL 35803

Website: www.tweetybirdaviary.com

Tel. No.: 256-656-2019

E-mail: LBroach487@Gmail.com

## Whidbey Birds

P.O. Box 1682 Coupeville, Washington 98239

Website: www.whidbeybirds.com

Tel. No.: 360-929-2869

E-mail: whidbeybirds@msn.com

## Birds Exotic

1060 S. Chester Ave. Delran, NJ 08075

Website: www.thebirdstore.com

Tel. No.:  856-764-2473

E-mail: thebirdstore@yahoo.com

## Birdmans Baby Parrots

5668 N Lincoln Ave Chicago, Illinois

Website: www.birdmansparrots.com

Tel. No.: 773-317-3785

## AJ'S Feathered Friends

804 N. La Fox Street. South Elgin, IL 60177

Website: www.ajspetshop.com

Tel. No.: 847-695-5624

## Something Cheeky

Clayton, North Carolina 27520

Website: www.somethingcheeky.com

Tel. No.: 1-919-585-2241

## In A Pickle Parrots

7924 Broadview Road, Broadview Heights, Ohio 44147

Website: www.inapickleparrots.com

Tel. No.: 440-627-6477

Email: Inapickleaviary@aol.com

## World of Birds

15 Perry Street, Chester, New Jersey 07930

Website: www.worldofbirds.com

Tel. No.: 908-879-2291

Email: worldofbirds@optonline.net

## Morning Glory Birds

West Hempstead, New York 11552

Website: www.facebook.com/glory.birds.7

Tel. No.: 516-972-3860

## Featherheads

Port charlotte, Florida 33948

Website:http://www.birdbreeders.com/breeder/13627/feathe

rheads-florida-port-charlotte-FL

Tel. No.: 813-679-4961

## Ginos Exiotic Birds

Blue Jay, CA 92317

Website: http://www.birdbreeders.com/bird

Tel. No.: 176-095-604-66

Email: Gmorrialle@gmail.com

**Fancy Feathers**

31 Roseland Avenue, Caldwell, New Jersey

Website: www.fancyfeathersaviary.com

Tel. No.: 973-403-2900

E-mail: ddargenio@gmail.com

**The Bird Lady**

17044 I-20, Lindale, Texas 75771

Website: http://www.birdbreeders.com/breeder/7816/the-bird-lady-east-of-dallas-off-of-i-20-TX/reviews

Tel. No.: 956-309-0750

E-mail: debinmcallen@att.net

**SpringOak**

Dripping Springs, Texas 78620

Website:http://www.birdbreeders.com/breeder/5561/springoak-dripping-springs-TX

Tel. No.: 512-630-1626

Email: sherylcoffman1@gmail.com

**The Parrots Nest of Maryland**

4508 G Lower Beckleysville Road, Hampstead, Mary Land

Website: http://www.birdbreeders.com/bird/

Tel. No.: 410-374-1636

Email: livesaybrian@aol.com

## Linville's Aviary

Miami, Florida 33174

Website:http://www.birdbreeders.com/breeder/2920/linvilles
-aviary-miami-FL

Tel. No.: 305-968-1536

E-mail: cerbyu@aol.com

## Avian Events, LLC

Conyers, GA 30094

Website: www. avianevents.com

Tel. No.: 770-500-2882

Email: tom@avianevents.com

## Lone Palm Aviary

Loxahatchee, Florida 33470

Website: www.lpbirds.com

Tel. No.: 570-730-1366

Email: jessica@lpbirds.com

## The Finch Farm Co.

Miami, Florida 33101

Website: www.thefinchfarm.com

Tel. No.: 877-527-5656

E-mail: jenna.thefinchfarm@gmail.com

## Ara Aviaries California

Agoura Hills Los Angeles, California

Website: www.aracaris.com

Tel. No.: 805-338-3549

Email: billysaylors6@gmail.com

## Ana's Parrots

East Stroudsburg, PA 18301

Website: https://www.facebook.com/PoconoAna

Tel. No.:  646-496-5005

E-mail:  poconoana@yahoo.com

## Parrotsrok

Skiatook, Oklahoma 74070

Website: http://parrotsrok.com/Home%20Page.html

Tel. No.:  918-289-8787

E-mail:  mandmok@sbcglobal.net

## The Parrot's Cove

New Iberia, Los Angeles 70560

Website: theparrotcove.com

Tel. No.: 337-519-3943

E-mail:  theparrotscove@theparrotcove.com

## 5 Oaks Aviary

Oklahoma City, Oklahoma 73150

Website: www.fiveoaksaviary.com

Tel. No.: 405-209-4312

E-mail: fiveoaksaviary@msn.com

## Debbie's Birdhouse

32 East Harrison Street Tunkhannock, Pennsylvania 18657

Website: www.debbiesbirdhouse.com

Tel. No.: 570-240-7268

E-mail: Debbie57@ptd.net

## Cindy's Parrot Place

Chesapeake, Virginia 23321

Website: http://www.cindysparrotplace.com

Tel. No.: 1-844-572-7768

Email: info@cindysparrotplace.com

## Linville's Aviary

Miami, Florida 33174

Website:http://www.birdbreeders.com/breeder/2920/linvilles
-aviary-miami-FL

Tel. No.: 305-968-1536

E-mail: cerbyu@aol.com

## Delorce's Bird Barn

Charleston, South Carolina 29429

Website: www.delorcesbirdbarn.com

Tel. No.: 8432161553 or 8438198618

Email: brendabrinson1234@gmail.com

## Toucan Jungle

Vista, CA 92084

Website: www.ToucanJungle.com

Tel. No.: 760-672-0127

Email: Chris@Toucanjungle.com

## Bill and Kennys Family birds

135 Terry Road Hartford, Connecticut 06105

Website: http://www.birdbreeders.com/breeder/26465/bill-and-kennys-family-birds-hartford-CT

Tel. No.: 203 441-0366

Email:billsbirdsnbeaks@gmail.com

## Kedzie Parrot Place

East Lansing, Michigan 48823

Website: www.kedzieparrotplace.com

Tel. No.: 517-204-3878

Email: kedzieparrotplace@hotmail.com

## Pet Paradise

35535 Euclid Avenue, Willoughby, Ohio

Website: www.petparadiseohio.com

Tel. No.: 440-942-9016

E-mail:info@petparadiseohio.com

## The Bird Hut

Nashville, Tennessee 37221

Website: www.the-bird-hut.com

Tel. No.: 615-739-0631

E-mail: midtnecho@yahoo.com

# Chapter Seven: Keeping Cockatoos Healthy

You as the owner should be aware of the potential threats and diseases that could harm the wellness of your Cockatoos. Just like human beings, you need to have knowledge on these diseases so that you can prevent it from happening in the first place. You will find tons of information on the most common problems that may affect your bird including its causes, signs and symptoms, remedies and prevention.

## Common Health Problems

In this section, you will learn about the diseases that may affect and threaten your Cockatoo's wellness. Learning these diseases as well as its remedies is vital for you and your bird so that you could prevent it from happening or even help with its treatment in case they caught one.

Below are some of the most common health problems that occur specifically to Cockatoos parrots. You will learn some guidelines on how these diseases can be prevented and treated as well as its signs and symptoms.

### Tracheal Mites

Tracheal Mites are quite common in birds because it can infiltrate the bird's entire respiratory tract and the severity of the infection can vary greatly. Birds with mild infections may not show any signs but severe infections may produce symptoms including trouble breathing, wheezing or clicking sounds, open-mouth breathing, and excessive salivation.

### a.) Cause and Effect

This disease can be transmitted through close contact with an infected bird and through airborne particles. It can also be passed through contaminated food or drinking water.

## b.) Diagnosis

It is quite difficult to diagnose if your Cockatoos has tracheal mites, veterinarians often recommend performing a tracheal swab to check under a microscope for further evaluation.

## c.) Signs and Symptoms

Common signs include sneezing, wheezing or difficulty in breathing. Continuous bobbing of the tail while breathing is also a sign that you Cockatoo may have a respiratory problem. Tracheal mites also overlap with a number of other infections that has the same symptoms, so you need to make sure you have an accurate diagnosis.

## d.) Treatment and Remedy

Medications are available to treat the disease, though dosage can be tricky and many birds die from tracheal mites. It is best to consult your veterinarian first before getting any treatment options available for tracheal mites.

Other common types of disorders and injuries in Cockatoos include:

- Constricted Toe
- Crop Burn
- Crop Punctures
- Dehydration

- Splay Leg
- Ruptured Air Sac
- Slipped Tendon
- Split Sternum
- Scissors Beak
- Sour and Slow Crop
- Sinusitis
- Salmonellosis
- Nasal Discharge
- Gout
- Beak and Feather Syndrome

## Protozoal Infections

### a.) Cause and Effect

Trichomonas and Giardia are common protozoal infections, these infections usually occurs during the breeding process of Cockatoos. It spreads through breeding colonies of Cockatoos.

### b.) Signs and Symptoms

These protozoa usually target the intestines and digestive tract of the birds, which then causes diarrhea. If you think that your bird's feces are sticky rather than loose, it's a sign that your bird might be infected. As a precaution, you should bring him/her to a veterinarian for a lab report to prevent the infection.

## c.) Treatment and Remedy

The treatment for birds infected consists of several anti-parasitic medicines that are fortunately available to the vet, after which, your vet will suggest you to make your bird undergo lab tests to monitor and ensure that the medicine killed the virus.

## Aspergillosis

It is a respiratory disease caused by the fungus called *Aspergillus*, which is found in warm and moist environments.

## a.) Cause and Effect

The microscopic spores of Aspergillus are an airborne transmitted disease. The fungus does not cause the disease per se but if your bird does not have a healthy immune system it can cause illness.

It increases the chances of the spores being inhaled by your bird if the environment has poor ventilation and sanitation, dusty conditions, and in close confinements.

Other predisposing factors include poor nutrition, other medical conditions in the respiratory system and prolonged use of antibiotics or corticosteroids, which eventually weakens the immune system. Aspergillosis is more common in parrots than other pet birds.

### b.) Signs and Symptoms

There are two kinds of Aspergillosis, it's either acute or chronic, both of which attacks the respiratory system.

Acute Aspergillosis signs and symptoms include:

- Severe difficulty in breathing
- Cyanosis (a bluish coloration of mucous membranes and/or skin)
- Decreased or loss of appetite
- Frequent drinking and urination

Chronic Aspergillosis symptoms include:

- White nodules appear through the respiratory tissue
- Large numbers of spores enter the bloodstream
- Infection in the kidneys, skin, muscle, gastrointestinal tract, liver, eyes, and brain

Other signs of Aspergillosis may include:

- Rapid breathing
- Exercise intolerance
- Change in syrinx (voice box); reluctance to talk
- Discharged and clogging of Nares
- Tremors

- Seizures or paralysis
- Green discoloration in the urates may be seen
- Enlarged liver
- Gout (painful, inflamed joints due to urate deposits)
- Depression and lethargy

## c.) Diagnosis of Aspergillosis

Aspergillosis is generally difficult to detect until complete diagnosis. Do not compromise respiratory infections, consult the veterinarian immediately.
Here are some of the tests that your Cockatoos need to undergo through for diagnosis

- Radiographs (a complete blood count)
- Endoscopy (used to view lesions in the syrinx or trachea)
- PCR testing for the presence of Aspergillus

## d.) Treatment and Remedy

Always consult a veterinarian first to know the right remedy for your bird. There are reports that the antifungal drug Itraconazole may also be toxic to Cockatoos parrots than to other bird species. Another antifungal drug called Amphotericin B may be administered orally, topically, by injection, or nebulizing. Consult your vet for proper guidance. Surgery may also be performed to remove accessible lesions. Supportive care is often needed such as oxygen, supplemental heat, tube feeding, and treatment of underlying conditions.

### e.) Prevention

Maintaining a good husbandry and diet can highly prevent outbreaks of Aspergillosis.

Below are some tips you can do to ensure that your bird is free from such a deadly disease:

- Keep your bird in a well-ventilated environment.
- Always clean the food and water dishes
- Thoroughly clean cages, toys, perches and other accessories at least once a month.
- Replace substrate (material lining the cage bottom) regularly
- Offer a good nutrition, such as the right combination of fruits, vegetables and seeds

## Psittacine Beak and Feather Disease (PBFD)

PBFD is a viral condition that is responsible for damage to the beak, feathers and nails as well as the immune system of infected birds. These are very common in parrots between 6 months and 3 years of age.

### a.) Signs and symptoms

PBFD typically affects the feathers of infected birds as well as its beak and nails over time. Here are some signs and symptoms that your pet might have PBFD.

- Feathers are short, fragile, malformed, and prone to bleeding and breaking. Birds may first lose their the white, fine powder produced by specialized feathers to help maintain feather health when this happens more abnormal feathers will eventually develop.
- Beak has become glossy rather than the more typical matte appearance
- Nails and beak becomes brittle and malformed
- Significant loss of feathers (as the follicles become damaged)
- Loss of appetite (especially in young Cockatoos)
- Regurgitation or continuous vomiting

### b.) Diagnosis

Veterinarians will likely perform a PCR test to confirm the diagnosis. This test uses advanced techniques to look for the virus' DNA.

Most of the time PCR only needs a blood sample, but your veterinarian may also need to take a swab from your bird's mouth and vent.

Other kinds of test may include:

- Complete blood count and a chemistry panel tests.
- DNA test for specifically for PBFD

### c.) Treatment

The majority of clinically affected birds will die within a few months to a year because there are no antiviral drugs available to fight the virus. Your avian veterinarian can only help keep your bird comfortable because this condition is painful for the bird and it also allows secondary infections to take hold. Some birds may survive for a few months they will ultimately die from this disease.

### d.) Prevention

The only thing breeders and pet owners can do to prevent this deadly virus is to take pro-active steps but since you can't help the birds mingle with other birds as they travel from wholesaler to retail pet distributors to your home the best solution is to have your bird examined by an avian veterinarian and allow diagnostic testing.

It is also wise to take your bird for a yearly exam to make sure it stays healthy. Yearly exams can catch small issues before they get worse.

## Avian Pox

Avian pox is the single deadliest disease that acquired by Cockatoos. It is caused by an Avian Poxvirus infection and it causes real damage to Cockatoos and scarred it for life.

### a.) Cause and Effect

The virus is usually transmitted through a direct contact with birds carrying the virus. Biting insects or any contaminated surfaces may spread the disease even further and may make the pain worse.

### b.) Signs and Symptoms

The thickening of the eyes by mucous membranes is a sign that your Cockatoos is a carrier of the virus. It manifests through a wet form of the pox that affects, mouth, gullet, and upper and lower respiratory systems.

### c.) Treatment and Remedy

Veterinarians typically recommend 10,000 units of Vitamin A which are given by injection. Antibiotics are also given to treat secondary infections and a Mercurochrome solution is given to treat their mucous-thickened eyes. Consult an avian veterinarian immediately.

## E – Coli

Another common illness that affects Cockatoos is a bacterium called E-Coli. It is very rampant among psittacine birds.

### a.) Cause and Effect

E-Coli is a gram-negative bacteria found in guts of birds that are considered abnormal; this bacteria is highly capable of causing diseases especially if it reaches into the bird's bloodstream, respiratory system, and reproductive system or if the carrier parrot is under a stressful situation.

### b.) Signs and Symptoms

Coliform infections are the main cause of deaths in most Cockatoos, the E-Coli bacteria weakens the bird's digestive and respiratory system most of the time. A sudden loss appetite and difficulty in breathing may be a sign that your bird is suffering from this bacteria.

### c.) Treatment and Remedy

Veterinarians usually have to determine first if these bacteria are the disease causing agents or merely a secondary infection through a culture testing before treating it with antibiotics or other necessary medicines.

**Proventricular Dilation Disease**

This disease is commonly known as Wasting Disease, it is also common among Cockatoos species. It is an inflammatory wasting disease caused by a virus called Avian BornaVirus (ABV), which is mostly found in Psittacine species specially in Cockatoos. It primarily affects the Central Nervous System and multiple organs such as liver, kidneys, heart, brain, peripheral blood vessels, lungs and gastrointestinal tract.

**a.) Cause and Effect**

It is classified as a sporadic disease that has a very rare kind of attack to a bird's immune system. Unlike other virus which attacks the whole cell then move to another cell, ABV does not destroy the cells which leave the infected ones very little damage. Since the cells are not destroyed the immune system cannot detect it and thus the virus stays within the bird for an indefinite amount of time, which eventually weakens the immune system and results in continuous infections throughout the parrot's life.

**b.) Diagnosis**

Avian veterinarians have difficulties in detecting the virus because of other infections it can bring to the bird's health. The ABV does not show-up in the test results and there are other viruses similar to ABV which may also lead in the assumption that the bird is not a carrier even if it is.

### c.) Signs and Symptoms

ABV is also an asymptomatic virus, which means that there are no signs that the bird might be infected or a carrier. However, sometimes you can notice it if your pet experienced instances of mild disorders such as moaning, feather-plucking or self-mutilation to severe illness such as head tremors, paralysis, seizures or other sudden sickness due to infected organs in the body.

### d.) Treatment and Remedy

Veterinarians classified the severity of disease and level of impact to different stages such as low-to-moderate symptoms to severe and chronic stages.

Parrots in the early stages are given treatment to prevent the virus from spreading and eventually curing it. Although, this virus can be controlled and has a remedy, it's important that your bird always goes for checkup and undergo medical tests every now and then especially if it was diagnosed with the virus before.

### Coacal Papilloma

It is caused by a virus infection similar to warts in other animals and it is transmitted through direct contact.

These tiny tumors usually appear in the vent area of a Cockatoo where it can eventually block the fecal area of making it hard for the bird to defecate if it grows large enough.

### a.) Treatment

The recommended treatment for this is a laser surgery. As a remedy veterinarians also advised owners to offer Jalapino peppers to prevent and control papilloma in birds. Consult your avian vet on the right amount of peppers to feed to your Cockatoos.

### Psittacosis or Parrot Fever

It is a zoonotic infectious disease caused by an unknown organism whose natural hosts are birds such as Cockatoos.

### a.) Cause and Effect

It is an airborne disease and it can also be spread via the bird's feces. This disease is highly contagious. Before acquiring a Cockatoo, it's important that your bird goes through a Psittacosis test because this type of infection can also potentially harm a human being.

**b.) Signs and Symptoms**

The worst thing about this disease is that it is asymptomatic, which means symptoms does not appear or cannot be detected easily, you will never know when it could happen and if the bird is a carrier. Nevertheless, watch out for these possible signs that your pet might be having Psittacosis:

- Difficulty in breathing (due to Respiratory infections with airsac)
- Sneezing
- Runny eyes
- Congestion
- Liver disease might occur (and can progress rapidly to death)

**c.) Diagnosis of Psittacosis**

As mentioned earlier, this type of disease is asymptomatic that sometimes even a psittacosis test could not detect the disease. Identifying organisms in the feces is done in most cases.

**d.) Treatment and Remedy**

This disease is treated with a tetracycline based antibiotic given for about 45 days to eliminate the carrier state, although some veterinarians believe that the antibiotic does not necessarily remove the carrier state.

## Pacheco's Disease

This disease is caused by a herpes virus which attacks the liver and results in acute liver failure. It is very contagious and highly fatal to most birds.

### a.) Diagnosis

Diagnosis is done via necropsy which detects microscopic evidences of the virus found in the liver.

### b.) Treatment and Remedy

Unfortunately, there is no guaranteed antibiotic or remedy for this disease, the best you could do is to minimize the spread of the virus through intensive care and some antiviral medication.

## Recommended Tests

Here are the recommended tests your Cockatoos should undergo through to detect potential diseases and further evaluate its health condition so that it can be prevented and treated as soon as possible.

For young Cockatoos, you might want to do a CBC or **Complete Blood Count**; this is a general test for birds and even humans to test for any internal infections. Another test is called **Chlamydophila Immunoassay**; this is a diagnosis exam to check if your bird might be carrying a contagious parrot fever, which is also potentially harmful to humans. You might also want to do a **Culture diagnosis** to detect if there are any bacterial infections in your young Cockatoos.

For adult Cockatoos, a CBC and Culture diagnosis should be done regularly as prescribed by your avian veterinarian as well as a full body X-ray usually with gas sedation for further evaluation of your pet's condition. If there are any signs of illness, veterinarians will recommend further tests to identify your bird's potential disease.

## Signs of Possible Illnesses

For you to keep your Cockatoos healthy, you need to monitor them to ensure that they are in good condition, however there will come a time that your bird will get sick. Here are some early warning signs that your Cockatoos could be potentially ill.

- **Activity** – Is your bird sleeping when it normally does not? Or being quiet when it normally isn't? Is there a decreased in food and water intake or not being able to eat at all like before?
- **Droppings** (feces) - Are there any change in urates

(white part) or feces that is lasting more than 1-2 days?

- **Diarrhea** - Have you found undigested food in your bird's feces? Their droppings should have the three distinct parts (green/brown, white and liquid urine). If you think your Cockatoos has diarrhea, contact your vet immediately.
- **Weight loss** - Does your bird feels "light" when you pick it up? That maybe a sign of weight loss because the Keel bone becomes more prominent.
- **Feathers** – Is there a continuous presence of pinfeathers? It may be dull in color, broken, bent and fluffed up feathers.
- **Sneezing** – Is there a discharge in the nostrils when your bird sneezes? Look for stained feathers over the nares or crusty material in or around the nostrils.
- **Vomiting** – Has your pet been vomiting for quite a long period of time already? Cockatoos and all birds regurgitate occasionally as a sign of "affection" but it could also indicate a crop infection
- **Respiratory** – Are there signs of respiratory distress like tail bobbing up and down with each breath, a change in breathing sounds, and wheezing or clicking noise when it inhales?

- **Balance** – Has your bird been falling off its perch and huddling at the bottom of cage? It is a sign that it's losing its balance.

- **Eyes** – Does it appear dull? Is there a redness/swelling and loss of feathers around the eyes?
- **Feet** – Is it scaly or flaky? Does it have sores on the bottom of the feet?
- **Head** – Have you noticed excessive head bobbing and shaking?
- **Beak** – Is your bird's beak swelling?
- **Behavior** – does your bird sits on the floor of its cage or habitat? Does it favor one foot over the other?

When these things happen, contact your avian veterinarian immediately. Do not compromise your bird's health; prevention is always better than cure.

# Chapter Eight: Cockatoo Checklist

Congratulate yourself! You are now on your way to becoming a very well-informed and pro-active Cockatoos owner! Finishing this book is a huge milestone for you and your future or present pet bird, but before this ultimate guide comes to a conclusion, keep in mind the most important things you have acquired through reading this book.

This chapter will outline the summary of what you have learned, the do's and dont's as well as the checklist you need to tick off to ensure that you and your Cockatoos lived happily ever after!

## Basic Information

- Taxonomy: phylum *Chordata*, class *Aves*, order *Psittaciformes*, family *Cacatuidae*, subfamily *Cacatuinae*, Genera *Probosciger, Callocephalon, Nymphicus, Calyptorhynchus, Eolophus, Lophochroa, Cacatua*
- **Distribution**: Australia, Indonesia, Papua New Guinea, Philippines, and the Solomon Islands
- **Habitat**: Shrublands, woodlands, rainforests, alpine forests
- **Lifestyle**: Flock Oriented
- **Anatomical Adaptations**:
- **Breeding Season**: between August to January
- **Eggs**: 2 – 3 eggs
- **Incubation Period**: – 25 - 30 days
- **Sexual Maturity** : 3 – 5 years old
- **Average Size**: 30 cm – 60 cm (12in – 24 in)
- **Average Weight**: 300 g – 1,200 g (0.66 lb – 2.65 lb)
- **Coloration**: white, pink, grey, yellow, black; different color mutations
- **Sexual Dimorphism**: not sexually dimorphic
- **Diet**: Seeds, Insects, Fruit, Nuts (Omnivore)
- **Sounds**: Vocal Communicator, Screamer
- **Interaction**: Highly Social
- **Lifespan**: 30 – 60 years

## Cage Set-up Guide

- **Minimum Cage Dimensions**: 27"x 27"x39" (70x70x100cm)
- **Cage Shape**: the bigger, the better. Never purchase a round cage.
- **Bar Spacing**: with 1 inch (4 - 5 mm) bar spacing **Required Accessories**: food and water dishes, perches, grooming and cleaning materials, cuttlebone, toys
- **Food/Water Dish**: 3 sturdy dishes; one for fresh water, one for pellet/seed mix, and one for fresh foods. Do not buy dishes made out of plastic
- **Perches**: at least 3 different perches; wood dowel, natural branch type, a therapeutic perch or a cement perch or any fresh fruit tree branches
- **Recommended Toys**: rotate at least 3 different toys; rope toys, stainless steel bells, swings etc.
- **Bathing Materials**: misting bottle; bath tub
- **Nests Materials**: nest box made out of wood, oak or metal
- **Recommended Temperature Range**: 65-75°F (18 - 24°C)
- **Lighting**: full color light bulb must be present in the cage area. Do not use incandescent or monochromatic light bulbs.

## Nutritional Information

- **Types of Recommended Food:**
- **Seeds:** 1/8 - 1/4 cup of fortified parrot seed mix
- **Fresh Fruits and Vegetables:** makes up about 15 to 20% of a Cockatoo's diet. Offer fruits and vegetables daily or every 2 - 3 days.
- **Supplements:** Calcium usually found in the form of a cuttlebone or Calcium treat. Powdered supplement such as packaged oyster shell can be added directly to your pet's food.
- **Amino Acids:** makes up about 20% of a Cockatoo's diet.
- **Carbohydrates:** makes up about 10% of a Cockatoo's diet (nuts, seeds, corn etc.)
- **Water:** clean, fresh and cool water; unflavored bottled drinking water or bottled natural spring water

## Breeding Information

- **Sexual Dimorphism**: They are not sexually dimorphic; gender can be identified through DNA sexing or chromosomal analysis.
- **Seasonal Changes**: breeding season usually begins in from August to January.
- **Sexual Maturity:** 3 to 5 years old

- **Nest Box Size:** for small cockatoos 12" wide x 31" high or (30 cm x 80 cm); for medium-sized cockatoos 14" wide x 39" high (35 cm x 100 cm); for large cockatoos 18" wide x 59" high (45 cm x 150 cm)
- **Hole Opening:** 4 in (10 – 12 cm) for small birds; 4 in – 5 in (10 – 12 cm) for medium-sized birds; 5 in – 6 in (12 – 15 cm) for large Cockatoos
- **Egg Laying:** female lays eggs an average of 2 – 3 eggs with an interval of 1 – 2 days.
- **Clutch Size:** about 2 – 3 clutches per year
- **Incubation Period:** 25 – 30 days
- **Hatching:** takes about 24 – 48 hours to hatch
- **Chick Independence:** 2 – 3 months (60 - 100 days)

## Do's and Dont's

- Do keep them busy and happy;
- Do feed them a variety of nutritious food
- Do train them well to maximize their intelligence
- Do provide a clean and healthy environment
- Do give them time and commitment
- Do care for them when they feel ill
- Do provide plenty of toys inside the cage
- Do bond with them and let them out of the cage once in a while so that they can be exposed outside

- Do not use sandpaper covered perches or floor paper. It can cause severe damage to your bird's feet
- Do not use "bird disks" or "mite disks". These may harm your bird. See your avian veterinarian if you suspect parasites.
- Do not use bird gravel. Bird gravel is used for birds that do not crack the hull or shell of the seeds they eat. It causes severe impactions, which are often fatal. Gravel only benefits doves and pigeons definitely not parrots
- Do not use negative reinforcement during training because it is not effective
- Don't let Cockatoos fall. It may contribute in developing respiratory problems and damages organs due to impact. Train them how to fly instead!
- Do not let your Cockatoos get near to the following household items to prevent causes of accidents:

  - Ceiling or electric fans
  - Cooking oil
  - Leg chains
  - Toxic Fumes
  - Wood shavings
  - Toxic houseplants
  - Pesticides
  - Lead or zinc materials

- Air fresheners
- Scented candles
- Sandpaper-covered perches
- Tobacco and Cigarette smoke

# Chapter Nine: Relevant Websites

Finishing this book doesn't mean that you should stop learning! This chapter provides you a wealth of references online that you could check out every now and then so that you can be updated when it comes to taking care of your Cockatoos. You can also find the websites you need to visit especially in buying cages and supplies for your pet.

*Cockatoos Cage Links*

Here is the recommended list of websites for you to choose from when buying cages both in United States and Great Britain.

**United States Links:**

**Custom Cages**

<https://www.customcages.com/catalogsearch/result/?o=Budgrigar+Cage&q=Cockatoo+right+Cage>

**Bird Cages 4 Less**

<http://birdcages4less.com/page/B/CTGY/Small_Bird_Cages>

**Bird Cages Now**

<http://www.birdcagesnow.com/Cockatoos/>

**Pet Solutions**

<http://www.petsolutions.com/C/Bird-Cages-Carriers.aspx>

**Pets at Home**

<http://www.petsathome.com/shop/en/pets/bird-and-wildlife/bird-cages>

## Overstock

<http://www.overstock.com/Pet-Supplies/Bird-Cages-Houses/3643/cat.html>

## Great Britain Links:

### Cages World

<http://www.cagesworld.co.uk/c/Cockatoo_Cages.htm>

### Northern Parrots

<http://www.northernparrots.com/Cockatoo-deptb103/?category=147>

### Pebble – Home and Garden

<https://www.pebble.co.uk/compare.html?q=Cockatoos+cage>

### Seapets

<https://www.seapets.co.uk/bird-supplies/bird-cages/parrot-cages>

## Cockatoos Cage Accessories and Supplies

Here is the recommended list of websites for you to choose from when buying accessories such as toys, perches, dishes and other necessary supplies for your pet.

**United States Links:**

### King's Cages
<http://www.kingscages.com/ >

### Doctors Foster and Smith – Toys
<http://www.drsfostersmith.com/bird-supplies/ >

### Fun Time Birdy - Toys
<http://www.funtimebirdy.com/patoyse.html>

### Pet Mountain – Cleaning Supplies
< http://www.petmountain.com/category/311/1/bird-cage-cleaning-supplies.html>

### PetSmart – Bowls, Feeders
<http://www.petsmart.com/bird/bowls-feeders/cat-36-catid-400014>

**Wind City Parrot - Accessories**

<http://www.windycityparrot.com/All_c_711.html>

**Pet Solutions - Breeding Supplies**

<http://www.petsolutions.com/C/Bird-Breeding-Supplies.aspx>

**Bird Cages 4 Less - Perches**

<http://birdcages4less.com/page/B/CTGY/Bird_Perches>

**Pets at Home – Health Care Products**

<http://www.petsathome.com/shop/en/pets/bird-and-wildlife/bird-healthcare-products>

**Overstock - Accessories**

<http://www.overstock.com/Pet-Supplies/Bird-Accessories/3646/cat.html>

**Great Britain Links:**

**Cages World - Accessories**

<http://www.cagesworld.co.uk/c/Bird_Cage_Accessories.htm>

**Parrot Essentials - Accessories**

<http://www.parrotessentials.co.uk/>

**Parrotize UK – Parrot Stands and Covers**

<http://parrotize.co.uk/products/parrot-stands/>

**Seapets – Bird Toys**

<https://www.seapets.co.uk/bird-supplies/bird-toys>

**ZooPlus – Accessories**
<http://www.zooplus.co.uk/shop/birds/cage_accessories>

*Cockatoos Diet and Food Links*

Here is the recommended list of websites for you to choose from when buying seeds and parrot food for your pet.

**United States Links:**

**Pet Mountain**
<http://www.petmountain.com/product/parrot-supplies/11442-609584/lafeber-classic-nutri-berries-macaw-cockatoo-food.html>

## Harrison's Bird Food

<http://www.harrisonsbirdfoods.com/>

## Nature Chest - Bird Food

<http://www.naturechest.com/bifoforinri.html>

## Petco – Bird Food; Treats

<http://www.petco.com/shop/en/petcostore/bird/bird-food-and-treats>

## Pet Supplies Plus

<http://www.petsuppliesplus.com/thumbnail/Bird/Food-Treats/c/2142/2162.uts>

## That Pet Place – Bird Food Supplies

<http://www.thatpetplace.com/bird-supplies/bird-food#!bird-food>

## Great Britain Links:

## Parrot Essentials UK – Vitamins and Minerals for birds

<http://www.parrotessentials.co.uk/vitamins-minerals/>

## Scarletts Parrot Essentials UK – Bird Food

<http://www.scarlettsparrotessentials.co.uk/food>

**Seapets – Bird Food**

<https://www.seapets.co.uk/bird-supplies/bird-food/bird-seeds>

**ZooPlus**

<http://www.zooplus.co.uk/shop/birds/bird_food/parrot>

**Bird Food UK**

<http://www.birdfood.co.uk/ctrl/node:114;page:2;/bird_food s>

**Ideal Price UK**

<http://www.idealprice.co.uk/compare.html?q=Cockatoos%20food>

**Northern Parrots – Parrot Treatments**

<http://www.northernparrots.com/treatments-and-cures-dept139/>

# Index

---

## A

accessories...........................................................14, 44, 45, 84, 130, 140, 148

animal movement license...............................................................................52

Aspergillosis.........................................................................127, 128, 129, 130

Asymptomatic.............................................................................123, 125, 126

Aviary...................................................................................................56, 57

---

## B

behavior...............................................................................11, 40, 41, 137

breeder..............................................................13,49,53,54,55,82,110,114,116

breeding........................... 11, 12, 109, 110, 111, 112, 113, 114, 115, 141, 149

brooding............................................................................................114

---

## C

cage....................................140, 43, 44, 45, 47, 84, 85, 86, 87, 88, 89, 92, 99, 130,
137, 140, 146

calcium...................................................................................100, 101, 141

CITES...........................................................................................50,51,52

clutch...................................................................11, 54, 111, 113, 114, 142

cost ...........................................................39, 40, 43, 44, 45, 46, 47, 48

cyanosis........................................................................................128

cuttlebone...................................................................100, 140, 141

---

## D

diagnosis ............................................................. 126, 129, 131,133, 134, 135

diet ...........................12, 46, 54, 89, 90, 93, 94, 95, 99, 100, 130, 139, 141, 150

diseases 13, 52, 94, 99, 113, 119, 120, 121, 135

dishes......................................................................44, 88, 89, 130, 140, 148

DNA.................................................................................11, 110, 131, 132

---

droppings............................................................................89, 113, 136

## E

E-Coli............................................11, 12, 99, 100, 111, 113, 114, 115, 139, 142
eggs....................................................................42, 85, 113, 127, 130
environment ....................................................17,37,39,44,69,70,72,82
eyes.............................................................20, 21, 82, 121, 125, 128, 137

## F

family............................................................................10, 12, 14, 139
feather..................................................9, 10, 40, 42, 82, 91, 99, 131, 136, 137
feeding....................................................................44, 46, 93, 94, 95, 130
female.............................................................11, 109, 110, 111, 114, 142
food....................46, 47, 48, 84, 86, 88, 89, 90, 94, 102, 136, 140, 141, 142, 150
fruits..............................................46, 90, 93, 97, 99, 102, 130, 141

## G

genus..............................................................16, 17, 18, 25, 26, 27, 28, 29
Great Britain..........................................................50, 52, 53, 78, 146, 147
grooming.................................................................43, 45, 91, 106, 107, 140

## H

habitat............................................................................12, 27, 85, 137, 139
handling ............................................................................91, 103
hatching ............................................................................114, 142
health....................................52, 54, 82, 86, 88, 89, 120, 123, 131, 135, 137
history ............................................................................7,23,55
hygiene...........................................................................45, 91

## I

illness...............................................................95, 121, 123, 127, 135
immune system...............................................95, 122, 123, 127, 130

incubation..................................................................11, 12, 111, 114, 115, 139, 142

infection............120, 121, 122, 123, 124, 125, 128, 129, 132, 133, 134, 135, 137

initial costs.................................................................................................43

---

## L

lay........................................................................................................142

license...................................................................................................52

lifespan................................................................................2, 11, 12, 139

longevity................................................................................................82

---

## M

male..............................................................................................109, 110

mating..................................................................................................111

maturity.................................................11, 12, 110, 111, 114, 139, 142

---

## N

nails.........................................................91, 103, 106, 107, 130, 131

nest.............................................................111, 113, 114, 115, 140, 142

nesting.........................................................................................113, 114

nutrients.........................................................................89, 90, 93, 94, 95

nutritional.......................................................................46, 93, 94, 141

needs..................................45, 46, 47, 84, 85, 86, 88, 91, 94, 99, 131

---

## O

oil..................................................................................................91, 143

order.........................................................................12, 85, 94, 112, 139

---

## P

Pacheco's Disease.................................................................................126

parrots.....................................2, 3, 8, 9, 11, 42, 45, 47, 90, 92, 94, 97, 102

PBFD virus..............................................................................................130

pellet..............................................................46, 89, 90, 94, 95, 99, 140

perches.................................................................44, 86, 88, 89, 130, 140, 142, 143
permit.......................................................................................................49, 51, 52
pet store.........................................................................13, 45, 46, 53, 54, 89, 107
prevention............................................................................119, 130, 132, 137
Psittacosis...................................................................................................125, 126

# Q

quick...............................................................................................12, 14, 15, 18, 105

# R

reproduction..........................................................................11, 110, 111, 113
respiratory.........................................91, 121, 122, 125, 127, 128, 129, 133, 137, 143

# S

seeds...................11, 12, 46, 89, 90, 93, 94, 96, 97, 103, 130, 139, 141, 143, 150
seed mix..............................................................................................89, 140, 141
sexing..................................................................................................11, 110, 141
sexually dimorphic.............................................................11, 12, 110, 139, 141
species...............................................9, 13, 106, 115, 120, 124, 127, 129, 130, 142
symptoms.................119, 120, 121, 122, 123, 124, 125, 126, 127, 131, 133, 134

# T

taming.......................................................................................................................104
training................................................................................102, 103, 105, 106, 143
temperature .................................................................................91, 92, 111, 140
toys...................................................................35, 43, 44, 45, 47, 89, 140, 142, 148
Treats...............................................................................................................46, 90, 102
treatment...................................47, 101, 120, 121, 122, 124, 129, 130, 132, 134
types.................................9, 14, 18, 35, 36, 37, 39, 41, 42, 47, 88, 90, 94, 141

## U

United States.................................................13, 26, 27, 50, 51, 52, 55, 116, 146

## V

vegetables.................................................46, 90, 95, 99, 130, 141, 127
ventilation.................................................................................. 127
veterinarian  .................................................91, 97, 99, 107, 108, 135, 137, 143
virus. ............................................... 120, 121, 122, 123, 124, 126, 127, 131, 132

## W

water................................................................86, 87, 88, 89, 90, 91, 101
wild ................................................................37, 42, 50, 88, 93, 94, 106, 113
wingspan.................................................11, 12, 19, 20, 21, 25, 28, 31, 32

# Photo Credits

Page 1 Photo by user Magnascan via Pixabay.com, <https://pixabay.com/en/cockatoo-sulphur-crested-cockatoo-583921/>

Page 12 Photo by user Barni1 via Pixabay.com, <https://pixabay.com/en/cockatoo-galah-australia-pair-649137/>

Page 23 Photo by user Kapa65 via Pixabay.com, <https://pixabay.com/en/sulphur-crested-cockatoo-1116179/>

Page 33 Photo by user ddouk via Pixabay.com, <https://pixabay.com/en/major-mitchell-s-cockatoo-parrot-ara-626313/>

Page 50 Photo by user Pruzi via Pixabay.com, < https://pixabay.com/en/bird-cockatoo-zoo-parrot-schopf-289222/>

Page 59 Photo by user Icb via Pixabay.com, <https://pixabay.com/en/cockatoo-parrot-bird-1521092/>

Page 75 Photo by user Myriam-Fotos via Pixabay.com,

<https://pixabay.com/en/cockatoo-white-pink-cage-together-1129586/>

Page 91 Photo by user Doug Janson via Wikimedia Commons, <https://commons.wikimedia.org/wiki/File:Probosciger_aterrimus-20030511B.jpg>

Page 111 Photo by user Sardaka via Wikimedia Commons, <https://commons.wikimedia.org/wiki/File:(1)Cockatoo_Centennial_Park-3.jpg>

Page 118 Photo by user Aviceda via Wikimedia Commons, <https://commons.wikimedia.org/wiki/File:Pink_Cockatoo_Bowra_Mar08.jpg>

# References

**"Breeding Your Cockatoo"** PetPlace.com
<http://www.petplace.com/article/birds/general/breeding-bird-reproduction/breeding-your-cockatoo>

"**Bringing Pet Birds into UK**" Jamescargo.com
<http://www.jamescargo.com/livestock_transport/PetBirdImport.htm>

**"Cockatoo"** San Diego Zoo Animals
<http://animals.sandiegozoo.org/animals/cockatoo>

**"Cockatoos as Pets: Personality, Care Requirements and Suitability"** BeautyofBirds.com
<https://www.beautyofbirds.com/cockatoosaspets.html>

**"Cockatoo Birds"** BirdChannel.com
<www.birdchannel.com/bird-species/profiles/cockatoo.aspx>

**"Cockatoo Care, Bird Care and Information for All Types of Cockatoos"** Animal-World.com
<http://animal-world.com/encyclo/birds/cockatoos/CockatoosProfile.htm>

**"Common Cockatoo Diseases"** BeautyofBirds.com
<https://www.beautyofbirds.com/cockatoodiseases.html>

**"Common Cockatoo Health Concerns"** Petcha.com
<http://petcha.com/pets/common-cockatoo-health-concerns/>

**"Disease & Health Risks"** Parrotparrot.com
<http://www.parrotparrot.com/parrot-health/disease-health-risks/>

**"Popular Pet Cockatoo Species"** by Alyson Kalhagen - About.com
<http://birds.about.com/od/breedsofbirds/tp/cockatoospecies.htm>

**"The Cockatoo Is A Cuddly But Needy Pet"** AllPetBirds.com
<http://www.allpetbirds.com/cockatoo>

**UK Breeders Listings**
<http://www.preloved.co.uk/>

**USA Breeders Listings**
<http://www.birdbreeders.com/>

Feeding Baby
Cynthia Cherry
978-1941070000

Axolotl
Lolly Brown
978-0989658430

Dysautonomia, POTS
Syndrome
Frederick Earlstein
978-0989658485

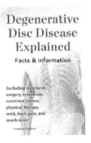

Degenerative Disc
Disease Explained
Frederick Earlstein
978-0989658485

Sinusitis, Hay Fever,
Allergic Rhinitis Explained
Frederick Earlstein
978-1941070024

Wicca
Riley Star
978-1941070130

Zombie Apocalypse
Rex Cutty
978-1941070154

Capybara
Lolly Brown
978-1941070062

Eels As Pets
Lolly Brown
978-1941070167

Scabies and Lice Explained
Frederick Earlstein
978-1941070017

Saltwater Fish As Pets
Lolly Brown
978-0989658461

Torticollis Explained
Frederick Earlstein
978-1941070055

Kennel Cough
Lolly Brown
978-0989658409

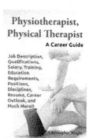

Physiotherapist, Physical
Therapist
Christopher Wright
978-0989658492

Rats, Mice, and Dormice
As Pets
Lolly Brown
978-1941070079

Wallaby and Wallaroo Care
Lolly Brown
978-1941070031

Bodybuilding Supplements
Explained
Jon Shelton
978-1941070239

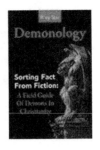

Demonology
Riley Star
978-19401070314

Pigeon Racing
Lolly Brown
978-1941070307

Dwarf Hamster
Lolly Brown
978-1941070390

Cryptozoology
Rex Cutty
978-1941070406

Eye Strain
Frederick Earlstein
978-1941070369

Inez The Miniature Elephant
Asher Ray
978-1941070353

Vampire Apocalypse
Rex Cutty
978-1941070321